Th

The Book to turn to
for Wisdom and Guidance

Michael Hurn
with Claire Hurn

For Brian & Candy

Life's Answers Lie Within

Michael Hurn

Claire Hurn

Eloquent Books
Durham, Connecticut

The I Ching, the Book to turn to for Wisdom and Guidance

This book is dedicated to everyone; who at some time in their lives (like ourselves), have found that they have had no-one to ask for advice or are in a situation that they would rather not discuss with anyone.

My heartfelt thanks go to Claire; for her love and support throughout the years that we have been working on this book, and for all the hours she has spent copy typing, editing, re-writing and generally for making my dyslexic words readable. Without Claire, this book would not have been possible.

Copyright © 2010: by Michael Hurn.

All rights reserved. No part of this book may be reproduced or transmitted in any form or by any means, graphic, electronic, or mechanical, including photocopying, recording, taping, or by any information storage retrieval system, without the permission, in writing, from the publisher.

Eloquent Books
An imprint of Strategic Book Group
P.O. Box 333
Durham CT 06422
www.StrategicBookGroup.com

ISBN: 978-1-60911-917-1

Contents

Introduction 5
How This Book Works 9
How to - Consult the I Ching 12
Worked Examples 15
The Trigrams 23
Your Notes 28
The Hexagrams 29
Bibliography 158
King Wen - Hurn, Lookup Table 160
How to - Summary 161
Example I Ching question sheet 162

The I Ching, the Book to turn to for Wisdom and Guidance

The I Ching is an ancient oracle that is still relevant and useful today. Consulting it is like asking a friend or mentor for their thoughts on your problem or situation. Anyone can consult the I Ching for themselves or for someone else who needs help or advice about any subject.

For over 30 years I have been studying, using, and introducing the I Ching to others. In this time, I have encountered various problems and issues. Hence my aim in writing this book has been to show respect for this ancient oracle while making it simpler for people to access its wisdom.

In traditional versions of the I Ching, look up tables are used to help you find your hexagram. In this book, I have simplified the layout and removed the need for look up tables. This as you will soon find makes looking up a hexagram easier than looking up a word in a dictionary!

Michael Hurn, Ottawa, Canada March 2010.

Acknowledgments

Once the bulk of the book was written, I gave draft editions to a few trial users/readers to test the layout and usability of the book. Therefore I wish to thank the following for their invaluable feedback:

Brian McCullough,
Cindy Muller,
Jacqui Ehninger-Cuervo,
Lori Holloway,
Sylvain Gagné.

Introduction

Everyone needs guidance at some time in their life. In today's busy world, your usual sources - Family, friends, church etc may not always be available to help. This is where the I Ching (the book of change) can be a useful source of comfort and advice that is readily available.

The I Ching is a valuable source of wisdom, advice and guidance. It can also give much needed hope while showing a way forward for those in despair.

The most remarkable thing about the I Ching is that you can ask it questions and that you will usually get a sensible answer. I say 'usually' because if you keep asking it the same question it will find a way to tell you to get on with life and to stop bothering it.

With the I Ching, questions need to be carefully phrased as it can't give straight yes/no answers. It will guide you as to the direction to follow, the right course of action to take. It does this by giving examples of situations in life and/or between family members.

You will find more details in the "How to - Consult the I Ching" section later in the book.

The I Ching is reputed to be the first book of recorded history; its origins date back to about 3000 BC. Over the centuries, with the input of many scholars the I Ching has become a treasure trove of wisdom. That is freely available for everyone who wants to use it.

In the eleventh century BC the I Ching went through a major rewrite at the hands of King Wen and his sons King Wu and the Duke of Zhou. King Wen is also credited with putting the wisdom of the I Ching into book form.

He did this by combining every combination of 2 Trigrams into Hexagrams[1]. This also gave the I Ching the core of its present day form. All traditional versions of the I Ching use the same numbers for the hexagrams.

The main problem with the King Wen sequence of the hexagrams is that it is not (to most people) an intuitive order.

---

[1] Trigrams are a stack of three lines, Hexagrams a stack of six lines; each line can be solid or broken.

The I Ching, the Book to turn to for Wisdom and Guidance

This makes it is necessary to refer to a look-up table to find your hexagram. (See the following example.) For beginners this can ruin an otherwise enjoyable experience with the I Ching.

	0	1	2	3	4	5	6	7
0	2	23	8	20	16	35	45	12
1	15	52	39	53	62	56	31	33
2	7	4	29	59	40	64	47	6
3	46	18	48	57	32	50	28	44
4	24	27	3	42	51	21	17	25
5	36	22	63	37	55	30	49	13
6	19	41	60	61	54	38	58	10
7	11	26	5	9	34	14	43	1

In this traditional look up table, the upper trigrams are across the top and the lower trigrams are down the left.

In this book I have put the hexagrams in 'line order'[2] and printed them onto the edge of the page. The Hurn[3] sequence both overcomes the problems with the King Wen sequence and transforms the way that the I Ching is used.

---

[2] This book makes use of a modified Fuxi sequence, composed by Shao Yung in about CE 1060.
[3] It would make the text of this book awkward to keep referring to it as a modified Fuxi sequence.

Introduction

Looking up a hexagram is now a simple matter of page flicking and pattern recognition. You work up from the bottom line, looking to see if the line is broken or solid.

The logic to this sequence is that broken lines come before the solid lines. This is also what that makes the new layout so intuitive.

The act of changing the order of the hexagrams has jumbled up the King Wen numbers. Digging into my background in computers, I have re-numbered the hexagrams in Octal. See the next section "How This Book Works" for details.

Chinese words can be very distracting for English speakers, especially when you try to pronounce them! Therefore, I have kept their use to a minimum.

In the world of the I Ching some would claim that, I should be writing about the Yijing. This is because Yijing is the Romanized[4], Chinese for "the book of change". Using the same logic I believe we should all be using zhōng guó or Zhōnghuá for China and zhōng wén for Chinese.

For the record the Chinese pronunciation of I Ching and Yijing is 'eejing' using 'ee' from 'feet' and 'jing' from 'jingle'.

The term 'I Ching' comes from the 1859 book *Peking Syllabary* by Sir Thomas Francis Wade. Sir Thomas was Cambridge University's first professor of Chinese. As this book is written in English, I feel that the use of I Ching is appropriate. (I take the view that 'I Ching' is the English translation of 'Yijing'.)

I have included details of two methods for consulting the I Ching. These are the traditional coin method and the dice method.

I devised the dice method[5] out of frustration with coins going everywhere when tossed yet again! My wife and I have also found that the very act of rummaging for the "right" dice; while thinking about the question helps us to relax and "tune in" to the I Ching.

---

[4] Romanize: to write or print (as a language) in the Latin alphabet <*Romanize* Chinese>. Yijing has been the approved spelling for 'the book of change', in international standard Chinese, (Pinyin) since 1979.
[5] The I Ching is very old and so are dice; so I will not be surprised if someone else has also come up with this idea.

The I Ching, the Book to turn to for Wisdom and Guidance

More details of both methods can be found in the "How to - Consult the I Ching" section later in this book.

Two important things in the process of divination are - how the inquiry is phrased and the act of writing it down[6]. These help you focus on what you want to ask and get you in the right frame of mind to do so.

Over time as you continue to ask questions, you will get better at focusing on what you want to ask and the answers will become more to the point.

In giving its commentary the I Ching will often refer to the superior man or members of a stylised family. This is not male chauvinism or prejudice; it is just a way to keep the phraseology simple.

Please remember that life is not Black or White, it is full of colour and shades of grey including black and white. It is like when you first talk to someone new who has a strong and unfamiliar accent. The more you talk to them, the easier it becomes to understand them. The more you use the I Ching the better your results will be.

When you come to use the I Ching you will find that some of the solid lines can change to broken and some of the broken lines change to solid. It is the changing nature of the lines and life that make up the heart of the I Ching (it is the book of change after all).

---

[6] When consulting the I Ching you can treat the Oracle as a friend who knows you well. Therefore there is no need to formally write down your questions.

How This Book Works

To understand 'How This Book Works' you need to bear in mind that the I Ching is made up of 64 Hexagrams. The Hexagrams are made up of every combination of 2 Trigrams. The Trigrams are a stack of three lines; each line can be solid (Yang) or broken (Yin).

Each of the Trigrams; represent the (stylised) workings of nature and named: Earth, Mountain, Water, Wind, Thunder, Fire, Lake and Heaven. Each Trigram has also been given associations that further connect it (and therefore us) to the world that we live in. See "The Trigrams" section.

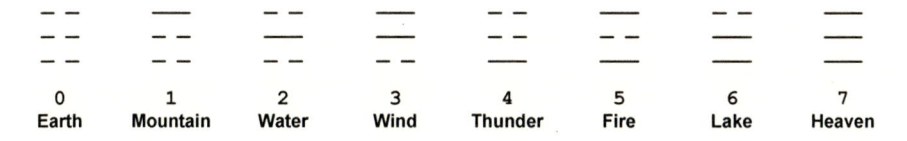

0	1	2	3	4	5	6	7
Earth	Mountain	Water	Wind	Thunder	Fire	Lake	Heaven

In much the same way that the I Ching groups three lines to form a Trigram. Early computer engineers would work with multiples of three binary bits[7], and use the Octal numbering system.

In Octal only the digits 0 to 7[8] are used to express all 8 of the possible combinations when you have three binary bits.

It is beyond the scope of this book to cover 'binary math' but the math can be extended to all six lines of the hexagrams. In decimal this would number the hexagrams from 0 to 63.

Re-numbering the hexagrams 0 to 63 has one major problem if you are given hexagram '6' you have to ask. Is it 6 in the binary order or 6 in the King Wen order? For the record 6 in the binary order is (45) in the King Wen order. Number (6) in the king Wen order is 33 in the binary order. So far everyone I have shown this to has got an instant headache! The only exception has been with my computer geek friends.

To overcome this problem I have exploited the fact that the hexagrams are made up of two trigrams.

---

[7] The Mainframe computers of the day used 36 bit words. Today they use 32, 64 & 128 bit words.
[8] In Decimal we count 0, 1, 2, 3, 4, 5, 6, 7, 8, 9, 10, 11 etc. In Octal you count 0, 1, 2, 3, 4, 5, 6, 7, 10, 11, 12, 13 etc.

The I Ching, the Book to turn to for Wisdom and Guidance

With the trigrams numbered 0 - 7 and putting the lower trigram first we get the hexagrams numbered from 00 to 77 as it stands this is not a complete solution since some of the numbers could still be confused with the King Wen numbers.

To remove any doubt I have extended the convention in octal to use a leading zero. Also for consistency to always use three digits. Thereby ending up with the hexagrams numbered from 000 to 077[9].

To provide a link with the numbers used in King Wen sequence they have been retained and placed in brackets. To give an example:

Conflict (6) 027: Lower trigram 2 Water, Upper trigram 7 Heaven

To show the change the following are the first 8 Hexagrams in the King Wen sequence.

(1)	(2)	(3)	(4)	(5)	(6)	(7)	(8)
077	000	042	021	072	027	020	002

The following are the first 8 Hexagrams in the Hurn sequence.

(2)	(23)	(8)	(20)	(16)	(35)	(45)	(12)
000	001	002	003	004	005	006	007

You do not need to understand binary, to use the octal numbering. But for completeness; the following is how I have used binary to give each trigram an octal number.

---

[9] In the world of computing it is standard practice to write Octal numbers with a leading 0. So a decimal 10 would be written as 012 in Octal. An Octal 017 is 15 in decimal.

Using the binary nature of the I Ching, solid lines are given a value of 1 and the broken lines a value of 0. This also shows that binary has been around a few thousand years before computers!

_ _ 0	___ 1	_ _ 0	___ 1	_ _ 0	___ 1	_ _ 0	___ 1
_ _ 0	_ _ 0	___ 1	___ 1	_ _ 0	_ _ 0	___ 1	___ 1
_ _ 0	_ _ 0	_ _ 0	_ _ 0	___ 1	___ 1	___ 1	___ 1

The next step is to turn the 1s & 0s 90 degrees clockwise.

_ _ 0	___ 1	_ _ 0	___ 1	_ _ 0	___ 1	_ _ 0	___ 1
_ _ 0	_ _ 0	___ 1	___ 1	_ _ 0	_ _ 0	___ 1	___ 1
_ _ 0	_ _ 0	_ _ 0	_ _ 0	___ 1	___ 1	___ 1	___ 1
0 0 0	0 0 1	0 1 0	0 1 1	1 0 0	1 0 1	1 1 0	1 1 1

Working from the left we give each binary bit a positional value in the sequence 4, 2, 1.

To convert from binary we give each 1 its positional value then add them together. We can now see the numbers used for each Trigram in this book.

_ _ 0	___ 1	_ _ 0	___ 1	_ _ 0	___ 1	_ _ 0	___ 1
_ _ 0	_ _ 0	___ 1	___ 1	_ _ 0	_ _ 0	___ 1	___ 1
_ _ 0	_ _ 0	_ _ 0	_ _ 0	___ 1	___ 1	___ 1	___ 1
0 0 0	0 0 1	0 1 0	0 1 1	1 0 0	1 0 1	1 1 0	1 1 1
0+0+0	0+0+1	0+2+0	0+2+1	4+0+0	4+0+1	4+2+0	4+2+1
0	1	2	3	4	5	6	7

How to - Consult the I Ching

Whether you use coins or dice, getting a good tumble is very important to ensure that the hexagram is random. When using dice, you also seem to get a better throw, and have more control over where they land.

Help with questions

When consulting the I Ching you can treat the Oracle as a friend who knows you well. Therefore there is no real need to formally write down your questions. So if all else fails it is OK to mull over your situation for a few seconds, rummage through your dice or coins and then just cast a hexagram.

Here are some suggestions for when you can't think of a question. You may also get some ideas from the worked examples later in the book.

How is my career looking?
How does my future look?
How is my health looking?
Are things likely to improve for myself / husband / wife / son / daughter?

Yes / no or either / or and multi-part questions should be avoided. It is best to ask about the effect of a particular action; the path toward a certain goal; the status of a specific relationship, and so forth.

Once you've formulated your question, it is helpful to write it down and date it. It should be short and concise. As you write it down try to see the question in your mind.

How to - Consult the I Ching

How to - Using Coins (traditional)

Find your "own space" - somewhere you feel comfortable and secure (could just be a quiet room).

While thinking of your question, select three coins from your pocket or purse. (Any like coins will do. Heads are valued at 3 and tails valued at 2.)

Write your question down on an I Ching Question Sheet or a fresh piece of paper. Keep thinking about your question as you toss the coins six times (once for each line).

The first toss gives the bottom line and so on upward. Much like the floors in a building the lines of a hexagram are numbered from the bottom/ground up. Each toss of 3 coins will give you a total of six, seven, eight or nine.

The six and nine lines are changing lines, when you get changing lines. The I Ching is giving its answer for the present with the first hexagram, and for the future with the second hexagram.

When you get changing lines you just draw draw a second hexagram to the right of first to show the changing lines.

A '9' line is a solid line in the first hexagram that changes to a broken line in the second hexagram. It is traditionally drawn as a solid line with an 'O'.

A '6' line is drawn as a broken line with an 'X'; to indicate that it becomes a solid line in the second hexagram.

See the table below.

Count	Line	First Hexagram	Second Hexagram
9	--O--	-----	-- --
8	-- --	-- --	-- --
7	-----	-----	-----
6	--X--	-- --	-----

The changing lines of the I Ching are what makes 'The Book of Change' such a versatile book for its students, helping them to unlock the wisdom and guidance within.

Flick the pages of the book to find your first hexagram. You will soon find that they follow a predictable pattern.

13

The I Ching, the Book to turn to for Wisdom and Guidance

Work up from the bottom line, looking to see if the line is broken or not; the broken lines come before the solid lines.

As you look up the hexagram disregard the Xs & Os and just think of broken and solid lines.

Read the main body text and the text for your changing lines (the lines with a 6 or a 9). Note: If you do not have any changing lines; just read the main body text as your situation is for the moment stable.

Flick the pages a second time to find the second hexagram but this time only read the main body text.

How to - Using dice

This method is very similar to the coin method so follow the directions above with the following changes.

As you throw the dice count the 'odd' numbers (1, 3 and 5) as 3 and the 'even' numbers (2, 4 and 6) as 2. Tip: Do NOT count the 'dots'.

I have been using the dice method for over ten years. In that time I have noticed that when a throw comes up with three of a kind (all 2's, all 5's all 6's etc.), that line has more relevance to the question.

When this happens, I draw a star by the line number as a reminder to pay extra attention to that line when reading the changing lines of the hexagram.

Worked Examples

The following examples are to help you "tune in" to the I Ching. As most users find they get more out of the I Ching after they have asked two or three questions.

Question 1: How is my future looking?

Background Info: The questioner has had a few years of uncertainly, but has just got the good news that his job security has improved.

```
    Line    Count    First Hexagram    Second Hexagram
     6        9        ——o——              ——  ——
     5        8        ——  ——             ——  ——
     4        9        ——o——              ——  ——
     3        9*       ——o——              ——  ——
     2        6        ——x——              ————————
     1        8        ——  ——             ——  ——

Hexagram number              015               020
```

Interpretation of answer: In the first hexagram the outcome looks favourable but there are a number of warnings to help guide the questioner in the future.

The subject should take extra note of the text in the third line. Do not act out of turn keep steady and all will be well.

A summary from the second hexagram is to take your time and consolidate your position.

The I Ching, the Book to turn to for Wisdom and Guidance

Question 2: How are things looking for our finances?

Background Info: Finances have been shaky on/off for years!

```
        Line    Count   First Hexagram    Second Hexagram
         6        8        ___  ___          ___  ___
         5        9        _____o_____     ___  ___
         4        7        _____     _____
         3        8        ___  ___          ___  ___
         2        7        _____     _____
         1        7        _____     _____

    Hexagram number              066               064
```

Interpretation of answer:

Things are good just now.

Sadly you do not realize how good.
Take time to smell the roses.

Don't give up working towards your future; there is hope for a better future.

Be aware that not everything has solid foundations - be on guard!

Keep your head down & be tactful, don't take any risks.

Worked Examples

Question 3: How stable is our future looking?

Background Info: We have had years & years of turmoil & uncertainty and in the light of husband's contracting I am wondering how firm / stable we are going to get?

Line	Count	First Hexagram	Second Hexagram
6	7	———— ————	———— ————
5	8	—— ——	—— ——
4	8	—— ——	—— ——
3	9	————o————	—— ——
2	8	———— ————	———— ————
1	6	—— x ——	———— ————
Hexagram number		031	061

Interpretation of answer:

A new beginning out of mess & muddle, mistakes have been made the good news is that they can be put right.

Take control of situation and remember that things will get worse before they get better. It's time to move forward decisively.

Prune out the bad stuff. Beware of hasty / thoughtless action!

Stay calm, be organized, and be tactful. Keep going somewhere specific & be sincere.

Consult someone wise.

The I Ching, the Book to turn to for Wisdom and Guidance

Question 4: Does it look like my child will grow up to be a bully?

Background Info: Phone call from teacher, child scratched another boy.

```
        Line    Count    First Hexagram    Second Hexagram
         6        6        ---  x  ---       ----------
         5        6*       ---  x  ---       ----------
         4        7        ----    ----      ----    ----
         3        9        --------o-------  ----------
         2        6        ---  x  ---       ----------
         1        7        ----    ----      ----    ----

    Hexagram number            010                023
```

Interpretation of answer:

Address the situation; focus on the present situation and not what will happen in the future. Use this situation as a teaching experience.

Don't be hasty & rush to resolve the situation it was dealt with already, let sleeping dogs lie. Ask for help on how to address this with my son.

In the future should this happen again if I were to use a bold approach it will work out in my favour but this solution may cause some grief.

Worked Examples

Question 5: Will my son be well balanced?

Background Info: This is a follow up from question 4.

```
Line    Count   First Hexagram
 6        7     ──────────
 5        8     ────  ────
 4        8     ────  ────
 3        8     ────  ────
 2        7     ──────────
 1        8     ────  ────

Hexagram number        021
```

Interpretation of answer:

You have asked your question now stop asking more about your son. When seeking guidance from my Son's Teacher, be concise and ask my questions once or I will insult and anger the teacher!

Author note:

There are no changing lines; hence no second hexagram. This indicates that the answer has been given and the condition is stable for now.

We have repeatedly found that if the same question is asked over and over again, this hexagram crops up.

It is almost as if the I Ching is telling you to stop bothering it with this question. You should show proper respect and gratitude to the oracle for the advice and make good use of it. It is an insult to the I Ching to keep asking it the same question.

The I Ching, the Book to turn to for Wisdom and Guidance

Question 6: Should we make changes and improvements in our house this year or consider moving?

Background Info: The house is cluttered and there is not much room for tools and home projects.

```
              Line   Count    First Hexagram    Second Hexagram
               6       8        ___  ___          ___  ___
               5       9        _____o_____       ___  ___
               4       7        ___  ___          ___  ___
               3       8        ___  ___          ___  ___
               2       6        ___ x ___         _____
               1       7        ___  ___          ___  ___

         Hexagram number            002                020
```

Interpretation of answer:

Allegiance – It is indicated that you will be successful and more focused if you are adaptable and persistent with the situation at hand.

Take well deserved rest, allow others to lead, then there will be no errors. Things could get ugly and stressful for you if you do not heed the advice.

Author note:

This is a multi part question it would have been better to ask two questions.

How are things looking for us this year with regard to making changes and improvements to our house?

How favourable would it be for us to move?

The interpretation of the answers will show which has the better outcome.

Worked Examples

Question 7: What is the best job for me?

Background Info: Work in day care - a former City employee.

Line	Count	First Hexagram	Second Hexagram
6	7	— —	— —
5	6	— x —	———
4	8	— —	— —
3	7	———	———
2	8	— —	— —
1	6	— x —	———
Hexagram number		000	042

Interpretation of answer:

Persist with what is right. Know what you want. – Health assistance role etc. Let go of unhelpful areas or people. Be calm, stay strong.

Second hexagram:
An obstacle lies in my path – do not stumble blindly and don't give up. Make plans to overcome the obstacle. I will probably need help to get over this problem.

5th line: Be calm and confident but move slowly – now is not the time for big change.

Author note:

Although it is not recommended to ask absolute questions of the I Ching, any question is a good question if the answer helps you to move forward.

However, we always need to remember that the I Ching does not give yes, no answers. Therefore you will have to interpret the answer accordingly.

It is better to draw up a short list of jobs and ask for guidance for each job. Then put a job with the most favourable outcome to the top of your list.

The I Ching, the Book to turn to for Wisdom and Guidance

Question 8: How are things looking for my Husband's business trip?

Background Info: We have been working on this project for a number of years and now my Husband has a chance to go overseas to promote it.

```
        Line   Count    First Hexagram    Second Hexagram
         6       7      _____        _____
         5       8      ____  ____        ____  ____
         4       8      ____  ____        ____  ____
         3       8      ____  ____        ____  ____
         2       7      _____        _____
         1       9      ─────o─────       ____  ____

   Hexagram number          061               021
```

Interpretation of answer:

My Husband needs to be careful what he does and how he does it. Simplifying his life and planning ahead are very important if he is to succeed in his endeavours. He also needs to stay calm, be patient, and show no anger or indignation.

It is good to have a destination in mind. He should be sincere and make an effort. Heed this advice and good fortune will follow.

Changing line: My Husband should complete his own obligations before jumping in to help others with theirs. He should carefully consider how much he is willing or able, to take on.

Correct persistence is good but don't keep asking the same question over and over. Be grateful to the teacher.

The Trigrams

Each of the Trigrams has its own unique set of references and attributes. These include a family member, a part of the human body that it represents some characteristics, a color and an animal. Each Trigram also represents a force of nature.

Think of these as sign posts or reference points that make it easier for us to relate to and understand the way the hexagrams have been interpreted. This information can also be used to give a more detailed and personal interpretation of the hexagrams you cast.

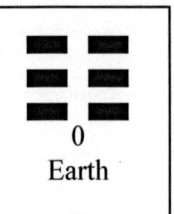

The I Ching, the Book to turn to for Wisdom and Guidance

0 Earth

Like a mother, the trigram Earth represents compliance, gentleness, encouragement and affection.

Earth can also be symbolic of the warmth, darkness and silence that you will find deep within the Earth.

Key:	Earth: fertility, passive.
Familial:	Mother.
Animal:	Cow.
Anatomical:	Solar Plexus (or belly).
Element:	Soil.
Colour:	Black.
Season:	Early Autumn.
Direction:	Southwest.
Abstract:	Compliance.

1 Mountain

Mountain is calm, meditative and sincere, able to retreat yet it has a very firm grip on reality.

The trigram mountain; can be thought of as a solitary person or a gnarled and twisted tree that tenaciously grows on a mountainside despite the conditions.

Key:	Mountain: arresting, stillness.
Familial:	Youngest Son.
Animal:	Dog.
Anatomical:	Hand.
Element:	Stone.
Colour:	Green.
Season:	Early Spring.
Direction:	Northeast.
Abstract:	Arrest (stopping motion).

The Trigrams

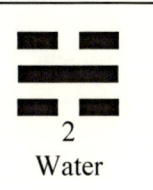

2 Water

The trigram water represents danger with all its hidden consequences and negative forces.

It is symbolic of soft, green wood – it soaks up water and possesses no useful strength.

Key:	Water: a pit, danger and chasm.
Familial:	Middle Son.
Animal:	Pig (or boar).
Anatomical:	Ear.
Element:	Wood.
Colour:	Red.
Season:	Winter.
Direction:	North.
Abstract:	Hazardous.

3 Wind

The trigram wind represents a combination of strength and flexibility with calm, tranquil undertones.

It is symbolic of a willow tree that bends in the wind and returns to shape without snapping.

Key:	Wind: wood, gentleness, penetration.
Familial:	Eldest Daughter.
Animal:	Cat (or tiger).
Anatomical:	Thighs.
Element:	Air.
Colour:	White.
Season:	Early Summer.
Direction:	Southeast.
Abstract:	Penetrating.

The I Ching, the Book to turn to for Wisdom and Guidance

4 Thunder

The trigram thunder represents joyful and spontaneous determination. It represents volcanoes and earthquakes.

This trigram also represents a fast growing shoot as it pushes upward to the sunlight.

Key:	Thunder: turbulence, awakening.
Familial:	Eldest Son.
Animal:	Dragon.
Anatomical:	Foot.
Element:	Grass.
Colour:	Orange.
Season:	Spring.
Direction:	East.
Abstract:	Movement.

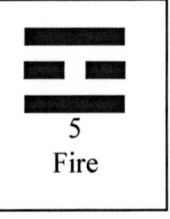

5 Fire

The trigram fire exhibits the attributes of brightness, warmth, beauty and cleverness.

It symbolizes trees that have become very dry and fragile.

Key:	Fire: brightness, beauty.
Familial:	Middle Daughter
Animal:	Bird
Anatomical:	Eye
Element:	Fire
Colour:	Yellow
Season:	Summer
Direction:	South
Abstract:	Brightness

The Trigrams

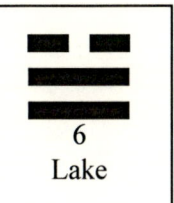

6 Lake

The trigram lake is like a mouth. It can be tender and sensual on the outside yet inside you will find it has a hard interior - the teeth maybe.

It also represents a temptress, fog, bountiful crop.

Key:	Lake: joy, purity and truth.
Familial:	Youngest Daughter
Animal:	Sheep
Anatomical:	Mouth (and lips)
Element:	Flesh
Colour:	Blue
Season:	Autumn
Direction:	West
Abstract:	Pleasure Satisfaction

7 Heaven

The trigram heaven represents energy and stamina.

It is also symbolic of extreme cold and the fruit of a tree.

Key:	Heaven: creative, active.
Familial:	Father
Animal:	Horse
Anatomical:	Head
Element:	Metal
Colour:	Purple
Season:	Early Winter
Direction:	Northwest
Abstract:	Strength

Your Notes

The Hexagrams

When reading the hexagrams read the main body text (on the left page) and only the text for your changing lines (the lines with a 6 or a 9).

Note: If you do not have any changing lines just read the main body text. This is normal it shows that your situation is for the moment stable.

If you are reading your second hexagram, the lines will have already changed so there is no need to read any of the text on the right page.

The I Ching, the Book to turn to for Wisdom and Guidance

Earth the Receptive (2) 000

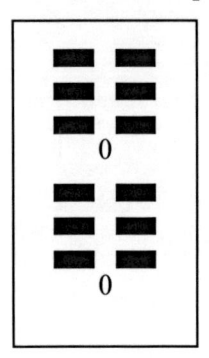

Upper and Lower trigram 0 Earth: fertility, passive.

Earth over Earth evokes; the warmth, darkness and silence that you will find deep within the Earth. Creative and feminine, this hexagram could also be associated with Mother Earth.

Heaven comes up with the ideas, earth makes them happen. The solution to this problem could well be a very creative and unusual one.

Wonderful progress, persist with what is correct. Know what you want to achieve but be aware that if you take the initiative you are likely to stray from the established path.

This is clearly not the time to take the initiative. Instead follow a leader for guidance. This does not have to be a physical person of authority. It could be a famous role model, a member of your family to chat to, your boss, a superhero. It does not matter who as long as it works for you.

It is good to find some like minded companionship and let go of unhelpful areas in your life be they people, thoughts or ideas. Be calm and stay strong.

The superior man takes no action but seeks guidance and makes plans for future activity when the time is right.

The Hexagrams

Earth the Receptive (2) 000

FIRST 6: Prepare for the worst and heed all warnings. Bide your time until the path is firm enough to walk upon or follow. Wait till the ice is thick enough!

SECOND LINE 6: Stop the pretences and deal only with the truth if you wish to succeed. The superior man proceeds toward his destiny as if pushed in the direction of a crowd rushing toward the exit.

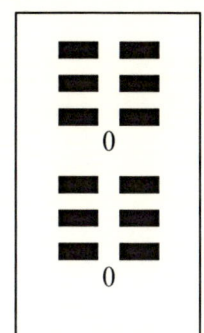

THIRD LINE 6: Knowing that your true virtue will eventually be noticed, you are content to work quietly in the background. Later on, your achievements and the progress that you have made will shine for all to see.

FOURTH LINE 6: Keep yourself to yourself be it alone or amid the world's turmoil. This is a time for caution; do not rise to the bait of the antagonists around you. Seeking un-deserved praise may be gratifying but will ultimately do you harm in the future.

FIFTH LINE 6: This is not a time to be boastful. Modesty about your inner worth will bring the greatest good fortune in the end

SIXTH LINE 6: Someone with a big ego fights to seize control. Unfortunately the fight will lead to serious injuries on both sides. Despite this, it is still possible to continue onward.

The I Ching, the Book to turn to for Wisdom and Guidance

Splitting Apart (23) 001

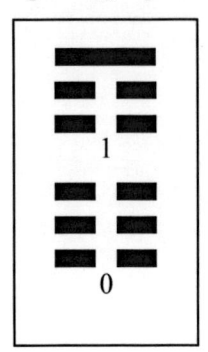

Upper trigram 1 Mountain: arresting, stillness.

Lower trigram 0 Earth: fertility, passive.

Mountain over Earth evokes; a landslide on a mountain falling back into the earth.

There is no advantage in moving in any direction. Face your concerns but stay calm. If possible, do nothing now but allow things to improve of their own accord.

Don't even think about taking on more obligations of any kind at the moment. Existing projects need to be kept ticking over until the time is right to move on them again.

The ruler (or boss) uses his wisdom, strength and experience to help and guide those below him. Everyone benefits from this arrangement as the people get the help they need and the ruler's position is strengthened.

The Hexagrams

Splitting Apart (23)   001

FIRST LINE 6: Something bad or unwanted has come into your situation and your position is being undermined. Even those you can trust are under the threat of misfortune. All you can do is accept what is happening and await the outcome.

SECOND LINE 6: At the present time, the utmost caution is required. You are in a bad situation with no allies to help you through. Great adaptability is called for in these circumstances. Taking a self-righteous stance will only lead to injury or worse.

THIRD LINE 6: He severs all ties with friend and foe. He is not to be blamed for being self reliant. Things will work out well in the end.

FOURTH LINE 6: You are in harm's way. Disaster is upon you and you are unable able to halt its advances. Defeat becomes a real possibility and you had no clue that it was likely to happen.

FIFTH LINE 6: A bad situation is getting better. Opposing forces are peacefully working together for a good cause that helps everyone. Success for all is now a possible reality. No grudge is held against him and it is advantageous once more to move in any direction

SIXTH LINE 9: The Superior Man has regained his influence once more and is respected by those around him. Those who are corrupt have been destroyed by their own negative actions.

The I Ching, the Book to turn to for Wisdom and Guidance

Working Together (8) 002

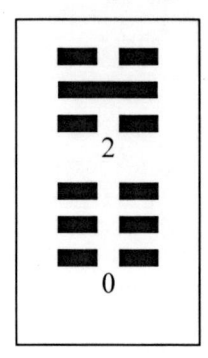

Upper trigram 2 Water: a pit, danger and chasm.

Lower trigram 0 Earth: fertility, passive.

Water over Earth; that men should work together to stave off the coming storm.

Uniting like streams flowing into rivers brings good fortune. A strong person is needed to hold the people together. If you give help to others they are more likely to help you in your time of need.

To confirm that your goal is correct, it is a good idea to ask the oracle again. From the new hexagram you will better understand how you can cope with the situation.

If the group is to flourish there must be mutual trust and respect throughout the entire group.

The leader of the group must have the courage to check that he can fulfill his responsibilities and obligations to the group. If he cannot, he must put the needs of the group fist and step aside for someone who can do what is necessary. His courage and honesty will bring good fortune.

The Hexagrams

Working Together (8) 002

FIRST LINE 6: Honesty, sincerity and integrity will attract others to you. This helps in the formation new and lasting associations.

SECOND LINE 6: Trust your own judgement and inner thoughts. Follow your instincts; be very careful who you associate with. Unexpected good luck comes your way.

THIRD LINE 6: The people you are associating with at present are not right for you. Being seen to be with them could do damage to your reputation in the future. Don't ignore them or antagonize them but open your heart only to those who are your equals

FOURTH LINE 6: You have the ear of a leader in your area. It is alright to openly support that person. However, you must remain true to yourself and ensure that you do not lose your own identity. Righteous persistence will bring good fortune.

FIFTH LINE 9: You are with people who happily work with you and support your goals for a better future. This friendly and relaxed working arrangement leads to great progress. Maybe fate had a hand in your meeting these wonderful helpers. Good fortune.

SIXTH LINE 6: Great misfortune – No venture can succeed if there is not strong leadership. The opportune time for unity has passed. Hesitation leads only to regret when it is too late.

The I Ching, the Book to turn to for Wisdom and Guidance

Contemplation (20) 003

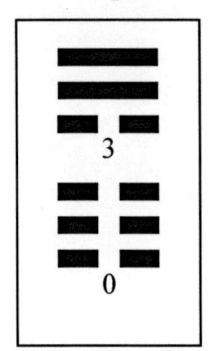

Upper trigram 3 Wind: wood, gentleness, penetration

Lower trigram 0 Earth: fertility, passive.

Wind over Earth evokes; the wind travelling the world.

All are touched by its breath yet it grasps not at all; it flits from place to place but cannot stay still or settle anywhere.

The Wind moves over Earth making the condition for Contemplating. One who is in a position to contemplate the rest of humanity should also expect to be looked at or scrutinized by the crowd. Don't let the thoughts of others concern you unduly. This is a time for inner contemplation without concern about what lies outside your window.

An ancient Chinese gateway erected high on a hill with its commanding view of the area for miles around is also a landmark that others can look at from far and wide. Some contemplate an object of great beauty and others will merely see an eyesore on the landscape.

The Hexagrams

Contemplation (20) 003

FIRST LINE 6: Only looking at how the situation affects you means that all you see is a tiny fraction of what is out there. For your own sake, open your eyes and take a look at the whole situation and how it affects everyone.

SECOND LINE 6: If you relate everything that comes your way in terms of your own life and attitudes, you cannot grow and develop as a person. It is time to look for something greater than you.

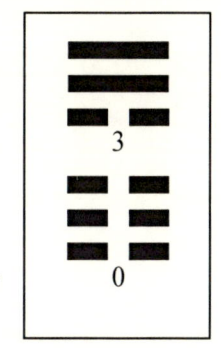

THIRD LINE 6: Take the time to step back and look at how others see you as you interact with the world around you. Do this and you will find your true self and gain the knowledge needed to move forward to a better future!

FOURTH LINE 6: It is now possible to move forward and make some progress by contemplating Society. Seek out the best leader or organization to throw your weight behind. You will be able to look beyond your position now and actually make a difference out there in the real world.

FIFTH LINE 9: Take a look at your own motives and how the way you live your life affects others. If you have been a good influence or role model to others then you will be able to enjoy a satisfying career with no blame.

SIXTH LINE 9: After much self contemplation, the man has managed to purge himself of all selfish interests. In so doing he is finally liberated from his ego. He can now think about moving on to better things.

The I Ching, the Book to turn to for Wisdom and Guidance

Anticipation (16) 004

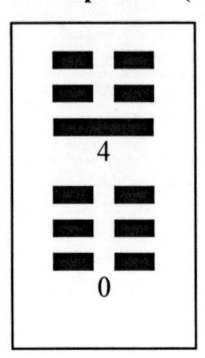

Upper trigram 4 Thunder: turbulence, awakening.

Lower trigram 0 Earth: fertility, passive.

Thunder over Earth evokes; the joyous beat of music played loud in celebration. It blasts out across the plain as people relax and enjoy themselves.

Although these are passionate and inspiring times it is important that actions are appropriate for the situation. Act with dignity and have respect for traditional values.

This is a good time to seek help from others. Your outcome could be unfavourable if you do not ask for help.

It is important that your supporters/helpers are briefed on the realities of the situation and your point of view. Then there will be no misunderstandings.

As the superior man gets used to being a leader, the people happily fall in line with his wishes.

The Hexagrams

Anticipation (16) 004

FIRST LINE 6: You have good relations with someone in a high position. It would be disrespectful to brag about it for your own selfish gains and gratifications. This would bring about self inflicted misfortune.

SECOND LINE 6: The superior man does not have any illusions, he sees things as they really are and does not waste his energies on un-necessary actions. He knows the precise moment to move. Keeping with this approach will bring good fortune.

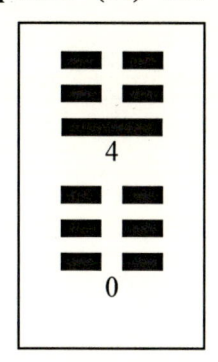

THIRD LINE 6: The man fails to understand that as well as looking upward to his goals, he must work hard at the appropriate time to make them happen. He who hesitates is lost!

FOURTH LINE 9: The Superior Man is happy, self confident and successful. Others are happy to work with him because it feels good doing so. Great success results from this happy working environment.

FIFTH LINE 6: He is very ill but does not die. He looks forward and finds that his way is blocked by obstacles at every turn. Being aware and mindful of this is what keeps him alive and moving forward.

SIXTH LINE 6: He is led astray by foolish thoughts of self gratification. However, a rude awakening and a positive change of course now even when all seems lost will save him. There is no blame.

The I Ching, the Book to turn to for Wisdom and Guidance

Progress   (35)   005

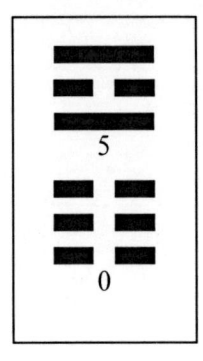

Upper trigram 5 Fire: brightness, beauty.

Lower trigram 0 Earth: fertility, passive.

Fire over Earth evokes; a procession moving onward across the plain with many torches lighting its path.

The Sun rises over the earth – A symbol of steady unhindered progress.

You have a lot of influence as to the outcome of the situation you are asking about, you just don't know it yet. Progress comes from one who is subservient to the Emperor (leader, boss or employer) but is also a leader or manager of others in his own right.

This person has considerable influence but does not abuse it. Instead, he uses it to serve the Emperor well and also for the good of himself and those who would help him. In so doing, his command of the situation is greatly enhanced. The grateful and enlightened Emperor showers him with gifts (promotion, pay rise, award…).

The superior man allows his virtue to shine brilliantly through bringing clarity to the receptive world around him.

The Hexagrams

Progress (35)   005

FIRST LINE 6: You try to move forward but are held back because your peers do not have faith in you or your abilities. Efforts are best spent honing the necessary skills to do the work well. Thus mistakes are prevented and you gain the confidence and respect of your peers. Do this cheerfully and wait out the delay.

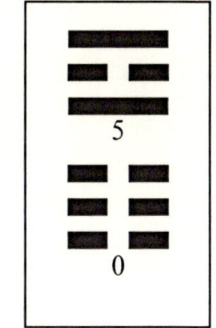

SECOND LINE 6: Frustratingly your efforts are not getting any recognition as yet. The only way forward now is to be patient and keep going with your efforts. Don't worry help is on the way. The symbolic "honoured Grandmother" (boss, friend, relative etc) comes to your aid with wisdom and guidance.

THIRD LINE 6: When you are sad you feel the need for encouragement and company to help you on your way and boost your flagging morale. Be assured that you will eventually feel better.

FOURTH LINE 9: Progress is perilous for the materialistic man and his hoard of dubiously acquired possessions. He has a goal in mind but is not able to reach it. Just like the Squirrel who sometimes forgets where he buried his food stash, the Man loses all that he has stowed away and is in danger of losing everything

FIFTH LINE 6: It is good to have a destination in mind. Don't be distracted from your goals by worrying about past mistakes, whether you will succeed or are you going to have problems and delays with what you are doing. Just keep moving forward with your plans and you will be successful.

SIXTH LINE 9: Strong measures and self discipline may be needed if you are to avoid mistakes. Such an approach; with others is not a good idea as they may take offence; leaving you lonely and humiliated.

The I Ching, the Book to turn to for Wisdom and Guidance

Gathering Together (45) 006

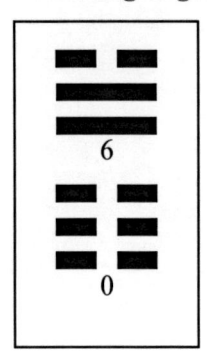

Upper trigram 6 Lake: joy, purity and truth.

Lower trigram 0 Earth: fertility, passive.

Lake over Earth evokes; the merging of many waters to form a lake and the hope and joy it brings to all.

A pool of water collects above the earth. The superior man organizes his weapons preparing himself for the unexpected.

Congregating together like a pool filling with water brings good fortune and success. It is favourable to watch the king as he wends his way to the temple. Sacrifices must be made to bring about good fortune. It is good to have a destination or goal in mind.

This is not time to be too self reliant. Family, friends and others are willing and able to help you work towards a goal or deal with a problem you are currently facing. All will be well for everyone if you take them up on it.

Share your own unique talents and gain the benefit of their knowledge, skills and talents. Good fortune will come to you, possibly in some quite sudden and unexpected fashion.

The superior man turns to the traditional guidance of his ancestors for a way forward that will work for all members of the group.

The Hexagrams

Gathering Together (45) 006

FIRST LINE 6: A crowd of people congregate to seek a leader. With so many different opinions being expressed, the situation becomes chaotic and confusing. A Cry for help will be heard. The people are calmed and unified by words of reassurance from their prospective leader.

SECOND LINE 6: This is a good time for going with the flow wherever it takes you. You will just know what feels right for you. Keep things simple and remember it is not the size of your sacrifice that matters but the sincerity and respect with which it is made.

THIRD LINE 6: The man finds the group he had intended to join with. He follows no direction and has no destination. Although upsetting for him he realizes that he would be better off following his own intuition and making his own choices. There is no blame in this.

FOURTH LINE 9: Great good fortune and no blame attached. A man brings people together to serve his prince (or boss or employers). What he does is not for him alone but for the good of all. His efforts are well rewarded with resounding success.

FIFTH LINE 9: A manager puts a team of people together. Some come to him only because of his rank or title, not out of faith in his abilities. He would be wise to cheerfully put them at their ease and gain their confidence by example - good leadership, work ethic, devotion to duty and so on.

SIXTH LINE 6: Sadness and tears but the blame lies elsewhere. There is always sadness when good intentions are misunderstood. He has not managed to bring the people together but it was not his fault. Therefore, he should not blame himself (or be blamed for it by others).

The I Ching, the Book to turn to for Wisdom and Guidance

Stagnation (12) 007

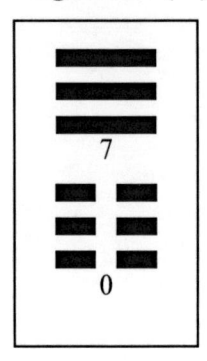

Upper trigram 7 Heaven: creative, active.

Lower trigram 0 Earth: fertility, passive.

Heaven / over Earth evokes: a messenger driven away because the message is not yet appreciated or understood by its recipients.

In this situation, things are still developing so it may be a good idea to ask the same question again in a few days time.

It does not matter who you are or how powerful you are, there is no advantage to be gained in this situation of stagnation. Heaven and Earth do not come together and so stagnation happens.

All is not what it seems in this confusing situation. Trust your own judgement, as those handing out advice may not have your best interests at heart. Stick to your own principles in this matter and steer clear of high risk situations which would be regrettable later.

The wise man knows when growing season is done for the year. He is calm and accepting of the situation and as a result is not unduly affected by it.

Stagnation (12) 007

FIRST LINE 6: It is time to change the environment you are in whilst being true to your own principles. If the necessary changes cannot be made now, it would be wise to retreat completely from the situation. If you do this, others who work with you may well go with you. Good fortune will come your way.

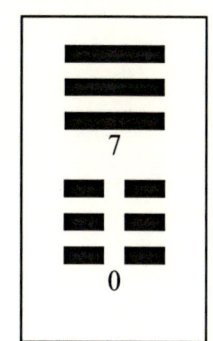

SECOND LINE 6: It is better to accept stagnation than to try to change the situation. In a time of stagnation even the wise man is unable improve matters. He just accepts the situation as it is, stays true to his principles and conserves his strength while waiting for the right time to act.

THIRD LINE 6: Power has been seized by questionable methods. Unfortunately the new leader has no power to over the people. He begins feel shame and self-doubt. With this realization comes a chance to put things to rights and improve the situation.

FOURTH LINE 9: An end to the period of stagnation is near. He responds to a sincere calling and is without reproach. His followers will benefit from this. Things are beginning to take a turn for the better. Like the prophets of old he leads his followers out of their stagnation and despair.

FIFTH LINE 9: Stagnation is at an end. Great changes for the better are showing up however; remain cautious for a while longer. In having such considerations, success is much more assured. Solid foundations are being dug for the good times ahead.

SIXTH LINE 9: Stagnation is at an end and good fortune comes. Stagnation does not just end all by itself. The people need a strong leader to guide them out of their despair and confusion. A state of peace is like a successful marriage, it requires constant efforts and a continuous sense of purpose to maintain it. Left un-tended, peace will slip away once more into stagnation.

The I Ching, the Book to turn to for Wisdom and Guidance

Humility - Modesty (15) 010

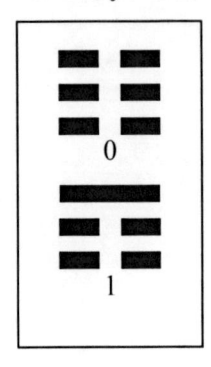

Upper trigram 0 Earth: fertility, passive.

Lower trigram 1 Mountain: arresting, stillness.

Earth over Mountain evokes; ants lowering a mountain.

As the ants move earth from its peak down to the plain below. The plain rises to meet the mountain as soil piles upward.

Be modest; stay realistic about your abilities and options in this situation. It is important to remember that if you become too arrogant and self important, you could lose valuable allies. Then the people will rapidly lose their respect for you.

A state of peaceful calm is best at this time. Little harm comes to those who can maintain their tranquillity despite storms raging around them. Great good fortune is the end result of quiet, stoic persistence in the chosen course of action.

The Hexagrams

Humility - Modesty (15) 010

FIRST LINE 6: A job well done, without fanfare or fuss ends in good fortune and great things. The superior man is modest about his achievements.

SECOND LINE 6: He who is modest receives true recognition. Persistence is the bringer of good fortune. Carefully maintain inner moderation and reap the rewards as your outer actions get you noticed. Success is at hand.

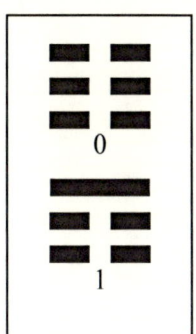

THIRD LINE 9: Although the superior man is recognized, he holds onto his humility. He humbly continues to work hard and be committed to the completion of his endeavours despite all that is going on around him. Good fortune is his. People are drawn to him because of his humility and work ethic. He has gained their support for future efforts.

FOURTH LINE 6: True equilibrium has been reached and must be maintained. True modesty comes with having faith in your abilities and knowing your position in life. Don't be boastful about what you have to others but respectfully ask them for help with carrying out your plans.

FIFTH LINE 6: Despite having reached balance in moderation, forceful action it may be needed to reach your goals. This should not be done with a boastful display of power but with fair and decisive action. There will be improvement in whatever you do.

SIXTH LINE 6: Your development is still a work in progress. Don't be tempted to blame others when things get difficult. Take responsibility for your own actions and order will come to your world. If you play fair and are just toward others around you your actions will be honoured.

The I Ching, the Book to turn to for Wisdom and Guidance

Keeping Still   (52)   011

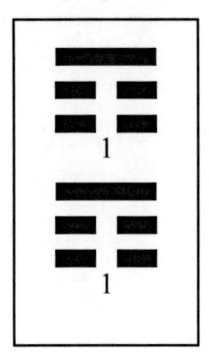

Upper and Lower trigram Mountain: arresting, stillness.

Mountain over Mountain evokes; the peace, tranquility and beauty of rock upon rock

The movement in both trigrams is completed creating stillness. It is time for meditation, stillness and quiet contemplation of the situation.

Move only when it is necessary to do so. The time to act is not yet upon us so for now focus your thoughts and efforts on the preparations for the move forward that is to come.

The superior man keeps his distance from the distractions of the outside world. Thus he is able to stay calm and composed both when by himself or with others.

The Hexagrams

Keeping Still (52) 011

FIRST LINE 6: The situation is only just starting up so it is not easy to things as they truly are. If you wish to advance you must stay positive and carry on being fair and objective then all will be well. Your ego is not yet big enough for you to trip over. It will be very good if you can keep it that way.

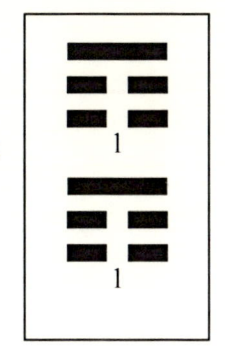

SECOND LINE 6: Danger, you are being swept along by events that you started up while blindly following a powerful person. This person you have been following is not acting with your best interests in mind. Stop and back off now while there is still time. Plan for damage limitation and what you are going to do next. Otherwise this situation will end in tears.

THIRD LINE 9: Trying force a restless body to be still could lead to inner pain and conflict. Take gentle steps to calm down, relax and meditate for inner peace and a more positive way forward to a better future.

FOURTH LINE 6: You are not yet free of doubt but you are well on the way to self mastery with your positive thoughts. You need to let go of your ego and its negative vibes to get the best out of your meditation.

FIFTH LINE 6: The way to true wisdom is instinctively knowing when to speak and when not to. Centre yourself and choose your words with care. Outspoken negative comments will be destructive to your cause.

SIXTH LINE 9: Gaining your inner composure will enable you to look beyond the situation and see things as they actually are. This will affect all aspects of your life positively. Good fortune will come from this honesty.

The I Ching, the Book to turn to for Wisdom and Guidance

Obstacles (39) 012

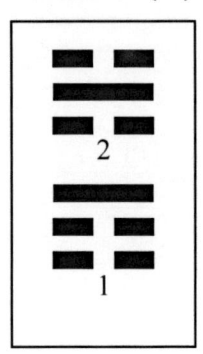

Upper trigram 2 Water: a pit, danger and chasm.

Lower trigram 1 Mountain: arresting, stillness.

Chasm over Mountain evokes; a path barred by a mountain glacier, dangerous and difficult to cross without the aid of a mountain guide.

Whichever way you choose will have many obstacles blocking the path. Don't give up, persistence brings good fortune. Your own strength alone will not be enough to overcome what lies ahead. Instead of fighting blindly forward ask for some help from an expert - could be a community leader/ tribal elder/ manager/ scientist…?.

You will put to good use what you have learned from the expert(s) as you plan for a better future when the time is right. Your persistence in what is right will be of great benefit not only to yourself but to those all around you in your community. Good fortune in the end.

The obstacle is not a permanent one and you will become a tougher person once you have worked your way through it.

The superior man knows that the only way he can overcome this problem is to be cautious. He takes the time and opportunity to examine his inner self and make the best of any useful assets he may find there.

The Hexagrams

Obstacles (39) 012

FIRST LINE 6: Do not go blindly forward. Stay where you are and carefully ponder the obstacles. You need to get a feel for their true nature and how to surmount them. The wise man will know when the time is right and when to move forward. All will go well because of all the planning and preparations.

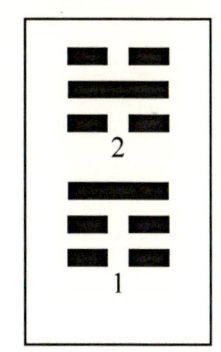

SECOND LINE 6: Obstacle after obstacle is encountered by one serving a higher cause. Obligation dictates that all obstacles must be faced head on and ways must be found to overcome them. This is the path of duty and an appropriate way forward for the situation. There should be no blame for this.

THIRD LINE 9: Struggling against an obstacle now endangers all. A father must not only think of himself but those he cares for. If he pushes forward now, he puts them all in the path of danger. In turning back to reconsider his plan, he is joyfully welcomed back by his family.

FOURTH LINE 6: It is necessary to rely on the help of others if you wish to succeed in meeting the challenge and overcoming the obstacles before you. A solo expedition will result in failure. Wait for the help to arrive then move together. Success!

FIFTH LINE 9: Despite the danger to himself, he has bravely gone to the aid of those who need his help. His brave efforts attract the help of others and he works with them to overcome the obstacles.

SIXTH LINE 6: Going forward is beset by obstacles. Standing still brings great good fortune. The time is right to seek the guidance of one who is wise and whose teaching can help all overcome. All is well.

The I Ching, the Book to turn to for Wisdom and Guidance

Gradual Progress (53)   013

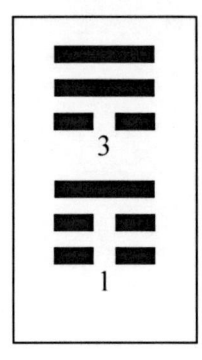

Upper trigram 3 Wind: wood, gentleness, penetration

Lower trigram 1 Mountain: arresting, stillness.

Wood over Mountain evokes; a gnarled old tree that grows slowly on a mountain top defying the harsh conditions it faces there.

Choosing to marry brings good fortune but sustained effort still needs to be put in to make it work for both parties.

Gradual progress is for the best right now. Avoid hasty actions and do not try to influence others to share your point of view. Bide your time, be flexible and allow the situations to come to fruition in their own time frame. Trying to change things too much now results in regret later.

The superior man realizes that improving himself and his virtues will be a gradual process as he slowly learns what is needed to make the changes.

The Hexagrams

Gradual Progress (53) 013

FIRST LINE 6: The younger son feels that he is in danger and pays too much attention to his critics and their gossip. Although there is criticism now, it need not lead to despair and disappointment. It can become a valuable tool to hone your skills and sow the seeds for future success.

SECOND LINE 6: Now that you are safe and secure, it is good to just be happy and share your good fortune with others. This line represents a successful marriage.

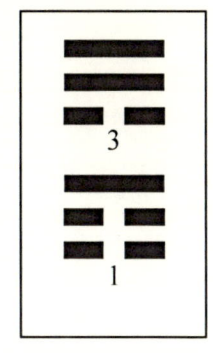

THIRD LINE 9: Misfortune results from bold advance and those you care about could be placed in harm's way. It is a better to let things to develop in their own time and make sure that what you already have is secure.

FOURTH LINE 6: It is important to be flexible now as you may need to be able move around obstacles and retreat quickly from danger. Keep safe now so that plans can be made ready for later success.

FIFTH LINE 9: As you gain more influence and power, you could be misjudged but people will eventually calm down and understand. Things will improve eventually.

SIXTH LINE 9: The geese are flying high – You will become role model or road map for others to follow as your achievements reach their highest peak. The greatest praise will come from those who admire and strive to copy you. Good fortune abounds for all.

The I Ching, the Book to turn to for Wisdom and Guidance

The Small Persist (62)   014

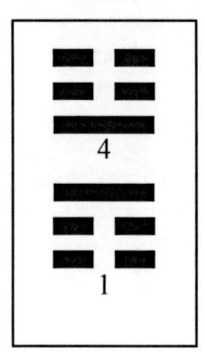

Upper trigram 4 Thunder: turbulence, awakening.

Lower trigram 1 Mountain: arresting, stillness.

Thunder over Mountain evokes; wise birds seeking safe refuge on the mountain as thunder rolls all around them.

There is progress to be made through Conscientiousness. The time is right for small things to be achieved. Now is not the time to become over ambitious. This is the time for small things getting done, minimal spending and conducting oneself in a respectful manner. With great things, remember, when birds fly high their song is lost.

The man who is promoted to a position which he is not ready for must be very careful. This is not the time to decide to make sweeping changes to the way you live, to begin bold new ventures or resolve major issues.

The Hexagrams

The Small Persist (62) 014

FIRST LINE 6: If a person has grand plans but does not do the groundwork and preparations, he courts failure and disaster. At the moment your destiny must remain with the plain and simple things in life. Great plans should only be considered when all else has been tried.

SECOND LINE 6: Now is the time to make use any connections you have to help your position. Remember that it is not how powerful the connection is that matters but that you have that connection at all. Be polite and stay true to traditional values in your dealings with them. No-one will be offended and all will be well.

THIRD LINE 9: Be prepared for the sudden danger or the possibility of unexpected threat from behind. Have an emergency plan ready to initiate at all times. Trust no-one.

FOURTH LINE 9: Slow and steady determination is best right now. Do not attempt to push ahead with your goals. Now is not the time to act. Danger lies ahead for the unprepared.

FIFTH LINE 6: You have the strength and power to get what you desire, but you are not able to do so right now. If you ask nicely for expert help from the right people you can still succeed in getting that which you desire.

SIXTH LINE 6: Anyone who tries to push forward with plans to reach an unrealistic goal courts disaster. Do so without thinking about the obstacles in your path and things will be even worse! Small things are still achievable at this time.

The I Ching, the Book to turn to for Wisdom and Guidance

The Wayfarer (56) 015

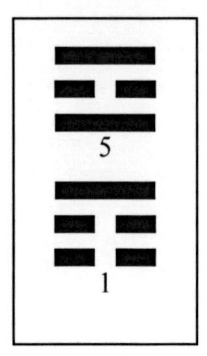

Upper trigram 5 Fire: brightness, beauty.

Lower trigram 1 Mountain: arresting, stillness.

Fire over Mountain evokes; the fact that nothing is permanent. A traveller lights a fire on the mountain but it will be gone when he moves on.

No fixed abode and an uncertain future sum up this situation. Yet you crave security and stability. Be patient, stay cheerful and have a sense of purpose and you will eventually gain that which you crave.

There will be Good fortune in small matters. Keep your mind firmly on what matters to you personally. Don't get involved in the squabbling and other issues of those around you.

Remember that while travelling you have to rely on the kindness of others for your needs. It is important that you show proper respect and gratitude for whatever they share with you. This is the time for humility, not bad manners and arrogance.

The Hexagrams

The Wayfarer (56) 015

FIRST LINE 6: If the wayfarer thinks only about the small stuff he will have a disaster on his hands. The wise man benefits from looking to the future and seeing the bigger picture. Mutual respect opens the doors to the groups and events you wish to get involved with.

SECOND LINE 6: The wayfarer quietly keeps to himself and behaves with dignity. This helps him to earn and keep the respect of others and he prospers materially. He also gains a follower who is loyal, helpful and trustworthy.

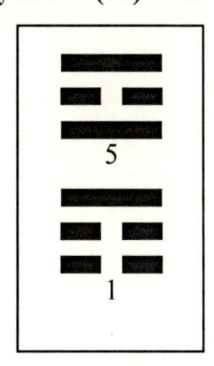

THIRD LINE 9: Rude and careless behaviour toward others will cost you what security you do have. The loyalty of those who have been there for you will vanish, leaving you in great danger with no supporters. Do not interfere in matters that do not concern you. Whatever your plans are, you would be foolish to proceed with them now.

FOURTH LINE 9: You know that you have almost reached your goals yet you have a feeling that you are not quite there yet. You feel insecure and lack confidence in the outcome. You know that you ought to move on but you feel protective of what you have already achieved. There is no feeling of satisfaction in what has already been accomplished.

FIFTH LINE 6: If you need to re-establish yourself; show modesty and generosity from the start. This sets you up for a long, fulfilling and rewarding life.

SIXTH LINE 9: Warning; do not become involved in trivial details that have nothing to do with your future development. They are merely a distraction on your journey.

The I Ching, the Book to turn to for Wisdom and Guidance

Influence / Attraction (31) 016

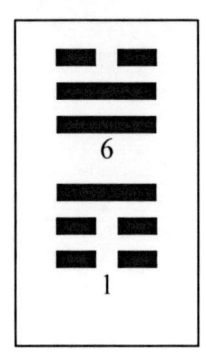

Upper trigram 6 Lake: joy, purity and truth.

Lower trigram 1 Mountain: arresting, stillness.

Lake over Mountain evokes; a mountain pool.

The pool's very existence makes the mountain beautiful and the mountain nurtures the pool. This is a perfect combination.

The influence of earth upon heaven and heaven upon earth give existence to all. The wise man influences the hearts of men and sees what causes pain and pleasure thus bringing peace and joy to the world.

Attraction comes in many forms and plays a very important part in our daily lives. In this hexagram marriage and the good fortune associated with it are mentioned specifically. It could also show the good fortune in other relationships e.g. business partnerships, friendships, Co-workers and so on.

It also plays its part in a variety of day to day situations you might be pursuing e.g. job hunting, house hunting, or angling for a pay rise. Correct persistence is advantageous now.

Whilst you may be enjoying or about to enjoy the pleasant things in life, don't allow the joy and excitement (or champagne bubbles!) to affect your judgement. Inner calmness and a clear head must be maintained. Listen to the advice of those you know and trust.

The Hexagrams

Influence / Attraction (31) 016

FIRST LINE 6: A tiny action could it be start of something new. Maybe an idea is not yet off the drawing board or a friendship. It does not matter right now as there is still a lot of work needed to make it real for others to notice it.

SECOND LINE 6: Make sure that you know what is going on around you before you take any action. Jump into the situation without thinking and you could find yourself in a lot of trouble and danger.

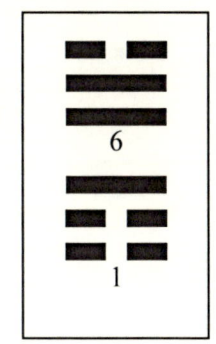

THIRD LINE 9: Self control is needed here so set limits and don't let your heart rule your head. This only leads to impulsive behaviour and embarrassment in front of others.

FOURTH LINE 9: Although now might be the right moment to act, take a moment to consider what lies ahead and how it is likely to affect those around you. Be consistent in all you do. Good fortune. However, if you leap without due consideration, there will be regret because it will become very difficult to convince others to follow you.

FIFTH LINE 9: To learn the depth of your influence on outside matters, take a good look within yourself. Make sure that your aims are not shallow and that they have strength of purpose and you will not regret it. You may have problems getting others to share your views. However, it is important to persevere.

SIXTH LINE 6: Talk is only talk and words are only words if they are not carefully thought about and there is no emotion to give them clear meaning. Ideas never come to fruition if they are not acted upon. Persuading others in this way leads to neither good nor bad fortune. So what exactly are you trying to achieve right now?

The I Ching, the Book to turn to for Wisdom and Guidance

Retreat   (33)   017

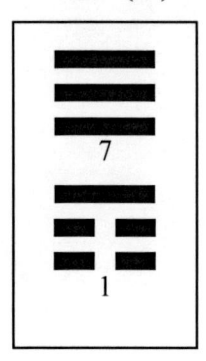

Upper trigram 7 Heaven: the creative.

Lower trigram 1 Mountain: arresting, stillness.

Heaven over Mountain evokes; the hermit retreats to the security of his home on top of the mountain.

Retreat should never be a disorganized and desperate struggle. Retreating when the time is right allows for an orderly and dignified re-grouping and preparing for the battle ahead. This is a sign of progress, not weakness.

It is good to keep going with small matters, but now is not a good time for action, even if you are defending yourself from the blows of fate or working on matters that concern you.

The superior man shows no anger and keeps his dignity. He steers clear of those who are not kindly disposed toward him.

The Hexagrams

Retreat (33) 017

FIRST LINE 6: Action now is not advisable. Planning a direction while in the action of retreating brings only confusion and danger. If only you had retreated earlier while there was still time to make plans - where to go, what to do next! Now it is too late and the enemy is nearly upon you.

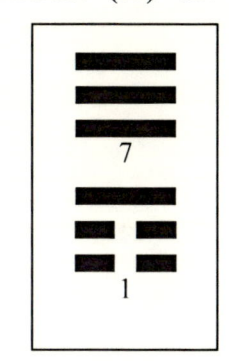

SECOND LINE 6: Retreat or escape can still happen if you work with wise and powerful friends on your side.

THIRD LINE 9: Retreat is delayed and this puts you in a difficult position. Although those around you seem to be keeping you safe, they are not helping to move the situation forward. Some might think that it is better to leave them to their fate and move on, but the superior man takes the initiative himself and leads everyone out of danger. That is indeed a step forward in the right direction!

FOURTH LINE 9: If a retreat is to be made, it is best done with a clear head that is free of emotional turmoil. Those who retreat while bogged down with emotional turmoil cannot think clearly and will suffer greatly, making bad decisions and poor choices that affect their future.

FIFTH LINE 9: Persevere and good fortune will be the result. Make the decision to retreat and keep firmly with it changing plans only as circumstances dictate. Be friendly and don't allow mere pettiness, debate and disagreements to disrupt your plans in any way. This is not the time for uncertainty of any kind.

SIXTH LINE 9: This is a happy time, retreat no longer holds any threat and there are no obstacles barring your way. There is no need for doubt or guilt. Labours and endeavours are successful and rewarded. Great good fortune comes your way.

The I Ching, the Book to turn to for Wisdom and Guidance

A Troop of Soldiers (7) 020

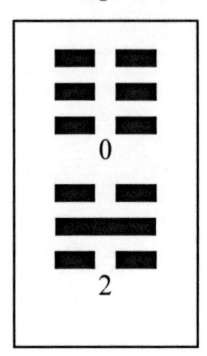

Upper trigram 0 Earth: fertility, passive.

Lower trigram 2 Water: a pit, danger and chasm.

Earth over Water; danger, a village has been built over a chasm that could collapse at any moment!

An experienced leader acts firmly and correctly, being fair and kind to the people while finding strength in their numbers. Watch and learn from him and you too could gain good fortune without reproach.

The only way to be successful is if you can organize yourself and your actions to be as efficient as a well trained troop of soldiers, always ready to move at a moment's notice. Now is the time for action that has been carefully thought out and planned. It is not the time for a thoughtless knee jerk reaction to circumstances. Work smarter not harder.

The superior man takes on the role of experienced leader. He treats everyone fairly, with respect and compassion. The people give him their loyalty and willingly work hard for him because they love him for the way he treats them. He achieves a lot.

The Hexagrams

A Troop of Soldiers   (7)   020

FIRST LINE 6: If there is to be any action it must be well organized and disciplined if it is to succeed. Action taken without any thought or planning is likely to end in chaos. Those who show good faith and lend you their support need to know that their efforts are appreciated.

SECOND LINE 9: The loyal troops respect the leader who fights with them in battle, sharing the rewards and victories with them. Follow this path - work or fight with your people or staff and success is assured. Don't try to stay safe or comfortable while others toil or fight on your behalf. Do so and you are likely to lose their loyalty and respect.

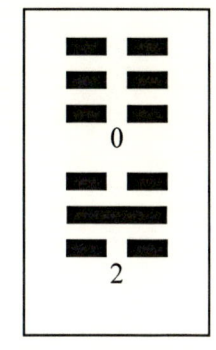

THIRD LINE 6: The inept leader has a big ego and over estimates what he is truly capable of. Things are bungled without good leadership. His troops suffer and there are losses. The fallen should to be honoured but this has to come after the needs of the living have been taken care of.

FOURTH LINE 6: There are many obstacles and a relentless enemy blocking the way, retreat is the only sensible option. The troop survives to fight another day. There is no shame in this strategic retreat.

FIFTH LINE 6: The time has come to defeat the enemy. The attack needs be decisive and well planned. This calls for an experienced leader and the element of surprise. An inexperienced leader is not the right person for this job but he can learn a lot from how the experienced leader plans for the coming battle.

SIXTH LINE 6: After the victory, the king rewards his army for a job well done. However, the rewards should be appropriate for the status of the individuals. The rank and file are not equipped to wield power wisely so do not give it to them.

The I Ching, the Book to turn to for Wisdom and Guidance

Youth Inexperience (4) 021

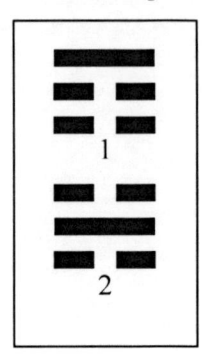

Upper trigram 1 Mountain: arresting, stillness.

Lower trigram 2 Water: a pit, danger and chasm.

Mountain over Water evokes; a tranquil mountain smiling down on its cool, wet foot hills as water flows all around.

Correct persistence is advantageous. When consulting the oracle however, it would be wise to remember that when a question is asked for the first time the answer will be appropriate and helpful but if you keep asking the same question over and over again, you can expect to get unhelpful answers.

The wise and experienced teacher is at first pleased to help and guide but as the question gets asked again and again, all that is being achieved is an angry and insulted teacher. Show proper gratitude and respect to the teacher for the advice and make good use of it.

The superior Man looks for the chance to bring out desirable qualities in both teacher and student. He does this without fuss or a desire to put himself in the spotlight.

The Hexagrams

Youth Inexperience (4) 021

FIRST LINE 6: The student needs guidance and discipline while learning. However, too much discipline could ruin the student's self confidence and passion for learning. It is important to get the balance of discipline just right.

SECOND LINE 9: The leader has been taught by the elders to have compassion and respect for his fellow man. He becomes a great and wise leader, who is loved, admired and respected by his people.

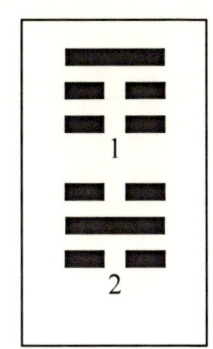

THIRD LINE 6: There is nothing useful to be gained by copying another. It is far better to come to terms with who you are and be happy with what you can achieve as a person. You have your own set of skills and abilities use them well, be true to yourself.

FOURTH LINE 6: The student is not realistic about his abilities and the teacher refuses to teach him anything more until the truth has been faced up to. This is one lesson the student must learn the hard way. Only then can the lessons resume.

FIFTH LINE 6: Simplicity in all things precedes good fortune. This is not a time for arrogance; the inexperienced should seek the teacher with humility and ask the question showing proper respect for the teacher. Accept and be thankful for the answer you are given.

SIXTH LINE 9: Punishment is not a means to an end but can be a good tool to show cause and effect for bad behaviour and nudge the student in the right direction. It needs be handed out in a clam, responsible way. If it is handed out in thoughtless anger, it could damage what good has already been achieved.

The I Ching, the Book to turn to for Wisdom and Guidance

The Abyss (29) 022

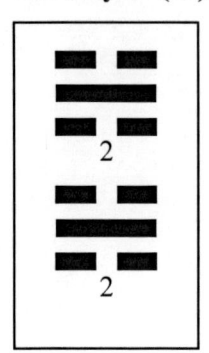

Upper and Lower trigram 2 Water: a pit, danger, chasm.

Water over Water evokes; danger inside danger, stress within stress.

This hexagram indicates danger on danger. Experiencing danger and adversity first had hones the mind, strengthens the spirit and shapes the character of a person.

It is very important just now to stay solidly tuned and true to your inner self and this in turn will help you to get a better understanding of the situation.

As stress and mental pressure build, they become the enemy. The human reasoning processes freezes into panic and a churning mix of emotions.

One must calm the mind to allow the body to act. Pass along the valuable lessons learnt from this situation that others may learn and benefit from them. To avoid disaster you must remain solid and reliable to the end.

The superior man is honourable in his conduct and teaches others with sincerity and dedication.

The Hexagrams

The Abyss (29) 022

FIRST LINE 6: Thoughtless action brings misfortune. You are lost but it would be a serious mistake to act before you have taken a moment to clear your thoughts. Having done this you can look back at the situation with fresh eyes and make plans for escape from this situation.

SECOND LINE 9: The danger being faced is very large and has many layers. It cannot be dealt with all at once. Calm yourself before taking another look at the danger. Mentally break it down into bite sized chunks that can realistically be dealt with one at a time. In this way, it is still possible to move forward.

THIRD LINE 6: When danger is not understood, it is best to stay calm and be still until you know what is going on. Actions should be simple and decisive. Don't waste your precious energies in movement anywhere until you have a solution to work with.

FOURTH LINE 6: There is no need to stand on ceremony. Be blunt and to the point, do not waste time wrapping the gift in many layers of pretty paper. Keep things nice and simple and keep a clear head. Useless clutter will only make an already problematic situation even more confusing.

FIFTH LINE 9: The danger will not pass of its own accord. Going with the flow and not being overly ambitious is the way forward. Over ambitious schemes and plans create more problems than they solve. The fact that you escaped is the main thing, how it was achieved does not matter.

SIXTH LINE 6: Although the danger is very real and for a time things will be chaotic, it will not last forever. Stop wasting your efforts on solutions that will not work. It is merely a matter of waiting it out and making plans for afterwards when it is all over.

The I Ching, the Book to turn to for Wisdom and Guidance

Dispersal (59) 023

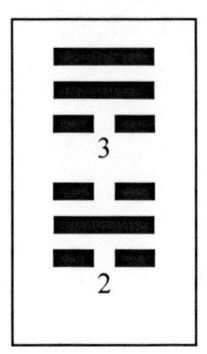

Upper trigram 3 Wind: wood, gentleness, penetration

Lower trigram 2 Water: a pit, danger and chasm.

Wind over Chasm; a breeze is capable of lifting waters from a gorge – It blows away the wet mist as it rises from the surface of the waters below.

Gentle Wind blows over the water. This is a time of progress and success. It is advantageous to re-unite with the collective flow. Single minded firmness and persistence are needed now for the time is right to cross the great stream. Gentleness releases pent up energies that have been bottled up for far too long.

It is important that you work with others on all areas of your life to help you succeed in your goals. Be calm and be kind in your thoughts and deeds with regard to your current situation and when planning for future ventures. This is not a time for mental or emotional rigidity. It is best to take things as they come. Don't hesitate or panic, stay focused on what you are doing!

If a mind is wandering it is not focused on the job. The end result is likely to be chaos! Stay focused on the task you are working on and all will be well.

The Hexagrams

Dispersal (59) 023

FIRST LINE 6: It is fortunate that you can clearly see the first signs of disagreement. This will make it so much easier to do what is needed to mend matters before they get out of hand.

SECOND LINE 9: Your inner feelings and negative emotions are the cause of your suffering. Your suffering can be avoided if you change your attitude towards those around you. Being more upbeat and friendly is all that is required to alleviate this situation and so end your suffering. Join in; don't hide inside your head!

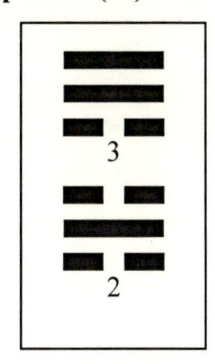

THIRD LINE 6: The task ahead is a very difficult one and it is necessary to stay focused. You must put aside all thoughts and activities that do not relate to the goal that lies ahead. In doing this, you will gain the strength to achieve great things. There is no regret.

FOURTH LINE 6: The time has come to let go of those people around you that hinder your progress toward the goal. Keep going by yourself and you will attract like-minded people who share your ambitions for the future. Great good fortune awaits you.

FIFTH LINE 9: Things are not going well, no-one can agree about anything. The continuing discord is putting the project in danger. Fresh ideas and a renewed sense of purpose are needed if people are to work together on solving the problem.

SIXTH LINE 9: Now is the time to use any means necessary to avoid danger for both yourself and those you care about. No-one will blame you if you decide to get away from the situation totally.

The I Ching, the Book to turn to for Wisdom and Guidance

Deliverance (40) 024

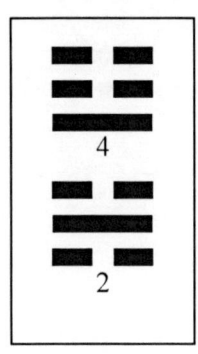

Upper trigram 4 Thunder: turbulence, awakening.

Lower trigram 2 Water: a pit, danger and chasm.

Thunder over Water evokes; the ride to freedom as we are delivered from danger. We go loudly, joyfully beating our drums heralding the way forward.

This hexagram represents Deliverance from dangers. Although the obstacles barring the way forward are now gone and troubles have been worked out, this is only a beginning. There is nothing to be gained by going forward now. So this would be a good time to take another look at positive ways of doing things that worked well for you in the past. This brings good fortune.

If you have something left to achieve be decisive and get it out of the way. Now is the time for boldly facing up to any problems in your life and clearing out anything that keeps you away from reaching your objectives. This is not a good time for new ventures.

No good can come from repeatedly brooding over past mistakes or regrets and the negative "what if" emotions associated with them. Stay cheerful and positive in all your actions and there will be good fortune.

The superior man forgives the errors of his opponents. He handles their transgressions with compassion and gentleness.

The Hexagrams

Deliverance (40) 024

FIRST LINE 6: Be thankful and take a break, the path has been cleared, the dead wood removed and positive progress can continue forward. This is the time to strengthen your position and heal your wounds.

SECOND LINE 9: The situation is being dealt with by others of lesser rank. Good fortune can still be achieved if you are honest and respectful in your endeavours.

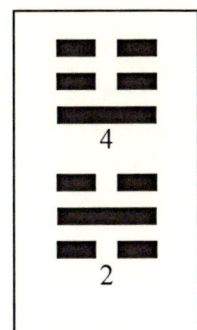

THIRD LINE 6: You have been promoted to a more powerful position but you don't have the right skills or experience to be effective. Put aside your pride and ask for the help and/or training you so badly need to keep going. If you don't ask, you will face misunderstandings and humiliation at the hands of others who would take your place. Things could get very ugly very fast as a result of your ignorance.

FOURTH LINE 9: Do not allow anyone to attach themselves to you to for their own selfish ends. Rid yourself of this excess baggage before those who share your beliefs and would help you in your efforts are squeezed out.

FIFTH LINE 6: You are the only one who can get yourself out of this situation. Once the leeches and hangers on have been detached from your person, you will win the respect that you deserve.

SIXTH LINE 6: If you are to get rid of your worst enemy forever, bold and decisive plans are called for. Timing is also critical. Once this has been achieved and the obstacle is removed from your path, you will succeed in your endeavours.

The I Ching, the Book to turn to for Wisdom and Guidance

Before Completion (64) 025

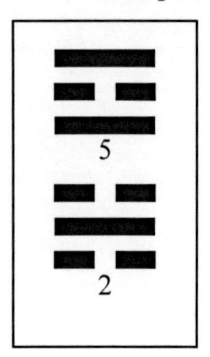

Upper trigram 5 Fire: brightness, beauty.

Lower trigram 2 Water: a pit, danger and chasm.

Fire over Water evokes; a man in mid leap over a chasm
He has not yet reached firm ground on the other side.

Just before the end, things are moving forward but despite all your hard work, the transition between order and chaos is still a work in progress. Don't feel defeated; keep working until the transition is complete. Be careful, for your progress can still be set back if there are any errors.

Success and good fortune through your efforts is still possible. However; this is not the time to take risks or be complacent. Do so and all your efforts come to nothing.

Before Completion (64) 025

FIRST LINE 6: The idea acting now to get something done while you still can is very appealing. However, now is not the time to make that move because cannot see the consequences of your actions. Taking action now can only lead to failure and humiliation on your part.

SECOND LINE 9: This is the moment to put the brakes on and wait until the time is right to make your move. Stay determined, keep your goal in mind and when the opportunity presents itself, jump on it!

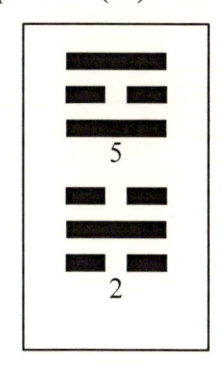

THIRD LINE 6: The time is right to move forward with your goal but you are not ready to do so. It would be an unfortunate mistake to move on this right now. It is better to work with others on a fresh start, moving only when you are better prepared to get the best out of this opportunity.

FOURTH LINE 9: In times of struggle stand firm and do not lose sight of your principles then there will be good fortune. Don't let anxiety and regret cloud your judgment as you fight this inevitable battle to its conclusion. Rewards come afterwards.

FIFTH LINE 6: The action was justified. The difficulties you have been facing have vanished in the face of your honest and determined efforts. Be happy and generous, the mission has been hugely successful. Now is the time to share your good fortune with those who have helped.

SIXTH LINE 9: The way ahead is going to be hard so by all means celebrate your progress so far but don't over indulge. You need to stay alert enough to deal with whatever crops up next along the way forward. Overindulge now and you run the risk of losing the respect of your followers and supporters.

The I Ching, the Book to turn to for Wisdom and Guidance

Exhaustion (47) 026

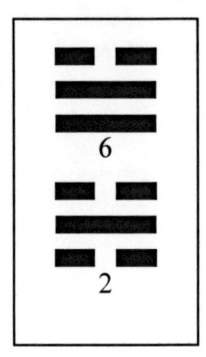

Upper trigram 6 Lake: joy, purity and truth.

Lower trigram 2 Water: a pit, danger and chasm.

Lake over Chasm evokes; water drains from the lake as a crack in the earth opens up under it, (almost as if someone pulled a plug out of a bath).

A pool of water has trickled away leaving behind a deep and barren chasm. Trees and plants are unable to grow and spread their branches. Where once there was joy, now there is emptiness.

Right now even the simplest things in all aspects of your daily life seem to be filled with difficulties you were not expecting. You are right; this is a time of adversity. However, you don't have to give in to the feelings of exhaustion and panic that come with it. You can turn it to your advantage, learn a lot and come out of this a better person. All you have to do is stay calm, be positive and cheerfully do whatever it takes to get out of this mess!

The superior man realizes that mere words and promises are meaningless unless they are acted upon and adhered to. He knows that it will take courage to continue with the struggles that lie ahead.

Be strong, be brave and keep going then there will be good fortune at the end of it all.

The Hexagrams

Exhaustion (47) 026

FIRST LINE 6: You are so overwhelmed by the problems that day to day life has taken a back seat. Sadly, you have lost the ability to step back and look at what needs to be done resolve the problems. Day to day life must continue while the problems are being dealt with. This is the only way out of this negative loop you are trapped in.

SECOND LINE 9: The good things in life can sometimes be too easily won. Boredom has become the enemy. Although now is not the time to make your move forward, Preparations for it would give you a renewed sense of purpose and would be a much better use of your time.

THIRD LINE 6: Your view of things has become distorted to the extent that things appear hostile and oppressive when in reality they are not. Wasting your energy facing obstacles that are not what they appear to be is a waste of valuable resources. Find out for yourself what is really out there.

FOURTH LINE 9: Don't be side tracked by the trappings of your new found wealth. Remember what needs to be done now. Although you may suffer some humiliation along the way, your strength of character will make it possible to achieve your goal.

FIFTH LINE 9: Your anger at the lack of useful information should not be allowed to get in the way of progress. Be assured that despite this lack of assistance, things will gradually get better of their own accord. You would be wise to spend the time calmly thinking about how to move forward when the time comes.

SIXTH LINE 6: Your judgement is faulty and clouded by how fearfully you have reacted in the face of past mistakes and adversities. How you deal with now and the future will also continue to be badly affected by this. Recognize your error; gain a more positive attitude and good fortune will follow.

Conflict (6) 027

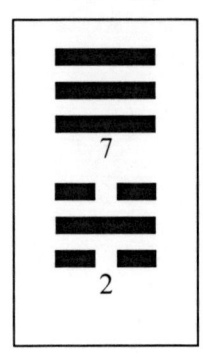

Upper trigram 7 Heaven: creative, active.

Lower trigram 2 Water: a pit, danger and chasm.

Heaven over Water; danger, the traveller needs to tread carefully; there is a chasm ahead that needs to be avoided.

In this situation you would be wise to stay calm and make careful plans for the beginning of the task. If you insist on getting your own way, there will be misfortune.

Caution and compromise is necessary if things are to get better. Keep a clear head and take a moment to consider all the implications in the situation about which you are asking.

Although it would be wise to seek the advice of a knowledgeable leader, now is not a safe time to cross the great water.

The superior Man realizes that he needs to be cautious and ask for help before he takes on a dangerous venture. So he looks for wise and experienced supporters to help him deal with his venture.

The Hexagrams

Conflict (6) 027

FIRST LINE 6: Conflict must be avoided or if it is too late, deal with it quickly squashing it before it bites too hard. Eventually this will all be sorted out to mutual satisfaction. All will go well but give it time.

SECOND LINE 9: Your enemy is a lot stronger than you are. Do not let false pride make you commit to a battle you cannot win. The wise man avoids disaster and retreats to fight another day. There will be no shame in this.

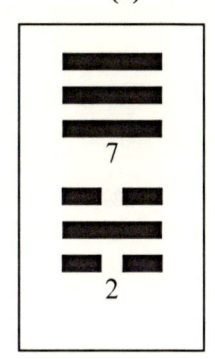

THIRD LINE 6: While serving others it is better to keep a low profile and be loyal. Remember, no-one can rob you of your strength of character as this is part of who you are. Be proud of that. Although position may be lost, there will be success in the end and conflict will have been avoided.

FOURTH LINE 9: You may not be happy with your situation. However the cause is unjust therefore fighting your way out of it is not the way forward. The superior man perseveres with what he has and finds peace and good fortune by working within the system.

FIFTH LINE 9: Getting involved in petty disputes that end in tears for both sides is not a way to resolve conflict. Instead, take your conflict before a just and powerful body for resolution. If you are correct and have nothing to hide, there will be success and good fortune in the end.

SIXTH LINE 9: Although you may gain victory in combat, you will not really win this one. It will end in an eternal challenge with no hope of a peaceful resolution. Where is the satisfaction in that?

The I Ching, the Book to turn to for Wisdom and Guidance

Moving Upward (46) 030

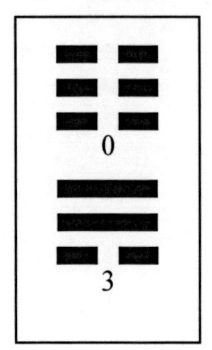

Upper trigram 0 Earth: fertility, passive.

Lower trigram 3 Wind: wood, gentleness, penetration

Earth over Wind evokes; a shoot pushing its way up and out of the earth toward the light.

Exceptional progress comes from moving forward. Seeking the leader is advantageous now.

This is a time for modesty and flexibility. You must act quickly as circumstances can change very rapidly. Ask those in powerful positions for their advice. Any guidance and assistance you are given will be extremely helpful in your quest to resolve the situation.

Moving Upward (46) 030

FIRST LINE 6: Despite being of lowly position, you are well liked and respected by your superiors. With hard work promotion is possible. You will become more confident in your abilities and within yourself as well. Good fortune.

SECOND LINE 9: Although your resources are meagre, you have sincerity that grabs the attention of those in authority. With their help you can achieve you goal.

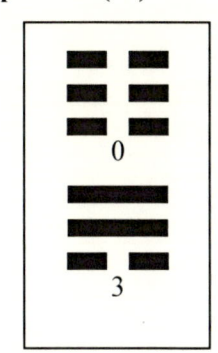

THIRD LINE 9: You are nervous because your move forward seems too good to be true. It is good to be cautious in case it was a trap. However, fear should not be allowed to stop you, keep going but watch your back.

FOURTH LINE 6: Things are very positive now as your success grows and your goals can finally be achieved. It is wise to stay true to your traditions and principles. Stick with what you know and understand.

FIFTH LINE 6: This is not the time to let your success go to your head. Stay calm, be careful and follow all the steps to the end. Good fortune.

SIXTH LINE 6: Right now you need to stay focused and determined. To do otherwise and blindly go forward leads only to failure, error and grief. With careful, determined steps, disaster can be avoided.

The I Ching, the Book to turn to for Wisdom and Guidance

Arresting Decay   (18)   031

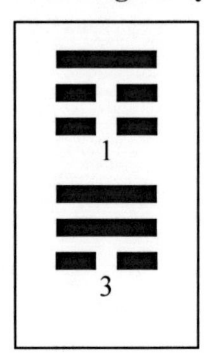

Upper trigram 1 Mountain: arresting, stillness.

Lower trigram 3 Wind: wood, gentleness, penetration

Mountain over Wind; a mountain valley carved out by centuries of wind wearing away the rock.

Out of chaos comes order. Once decay has arrested there can be a new beginning When de- cluttering a house, the mess and confusion is truly awful at first but once the clutter leaves the premises and better storage solutions are initiated for what remains, order reigns supreme.

The situation you are asking about has become very messy with bad decisions and mistakes made. The damage can be repaired by regaining control of the situation and taking the appropriate action. This will not be an easy task but the end result is worth the effort.

It is advantageous to cross the great water, moving forward with issues that concern you. A fresh start is coming. Be decisive in business dealings and remember that things often get worse before they get better.

This is symbolic of important power. Hard work is indicated but when all is completed there will be major success.

Arresting Decay (18) 031

FIRST LINE 6: If you wish to grow and be successful, some pruning must be done in your life. The rigid and traditional way you have been running your life is choking you. Beware, roses have sharp thorns! Be careful and respectful as you make the necessary changes and all will be well.

SECOND LINE 9: He repairs the mistakes of his Mother. Although you know that mistakes made in the past have to be rectified, take care not to hurt those you care about in the process. Be gentle, kind and considerate as you put things to rights. Things are not black and white here; the original error was not made deliberately or with malice.

THIRD LINE 9: The Son repairs the mistakes of the Father. You are anxious to rectify the mistakes of the past and move vigorously into the future. Your actions may be hurried and others accuse you of being thoughtless with regard the feelings of others. However, you will not be harmed by this.

FOURTH LINE 6: The son lacks the confidence to right the mistakes of his Father. Unfortunately the people see this as a sign that he does not care enough deal with the mistakes of the past. The decay and humiliation started by the Father's mistakes continues on and the Son is disgraced as well.

FIFTH LINE 6: The Son (now the ruler) accepts the fact that his Father was less than perfect. He takes responsibility for repairing the damage his Father's mistakes caused. The people proclaim him a true leader.

SIXTH LINE 9: The situation can be transcended. It is appropriate to withdraw from worldly affairs when the goal is spiritual. A Sage does not save the present but creates values for others to live by and in so doing, creates a better future for all.

The I Ching, the Book to turn to for Wisdom and Guidance

The Well   (48)   032

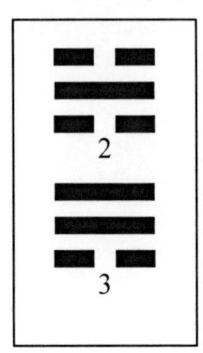

Upper trigram 2 Water: a pit, danger and chasm.

Lower trigram 3 Wind: wood, gentleness, penetration

Chasm over Wood evokes; a well bucket - when in good repair it will give water to all who need it. If it is broken there will only be thirst and frustration.

Now is the time to learn from the past, yours (the good and the bad) and centuries of mankind's rich legacy of wisdom, history and traditions.

The well source is eternal and can be tapped into again and again by those who need it. Every now and then there will be someone who finds that the rope is too short to reach the water or that the well bucket is broken.

This is symbolic of a goal nearly realised being snatched away at the last moment, misfortune. It takes a lot of hard work to achieve a goal, and one must keep up their efforts to the very end or it will be lost.

An enlightened person gently encourages those around him to work together to fix the leaks and generally deal with the situation. To help this process, he gives them the benefit of his wisdom and guidance.

The Hexagrams

The Well (48) 032

FIRST LINE 6: If a man is shallow and has no spark of enthusiasm for life, he will not be able to offer insight and encouragement to others who need it. They will quickly tire of him and He will be alone. History will not remember him.

SECOND LINE 9: You may have great abilities but if you are not using them regularly they will dissipate unnoticed. Sadly, when you really need them they could well be long gone and nothing can be accomplished. Use it or lose it.

THIRD LINE 9: You are very talented but your talents are not being used for the good of anyone just now. It is sad that no-one has noticed your talent. Recognition from someone who is wise, powerful and able to put your talent to work for the good of everyone brings good fortune.

FOURTH LINE 6: Your personal goals need to be re-evaluated before you can continue on the journey of life. Right now you would be wise to put getting your life in order at the top of your to do list. Sadly this means that you cannot help anybody else with their problems at this time. Don't feel guilty. You will be able to help them later once you are sorted.

FIFTH LINE 9: You are very wise and have much to offer others. However, right now, your own issues in daily life and future development need to come first.

SIXTH LINE 6: Now is the time to share your bounty of wisdom, advice and guidance with others. The more people you help, the stronger your spiritual wisdom and wealth becomes. Supreme good fortune is yours now, you have earned it.

The I Ching, the Book to turn to for Wisdom and Guidance

Gentleness - Penetration   (57)   033

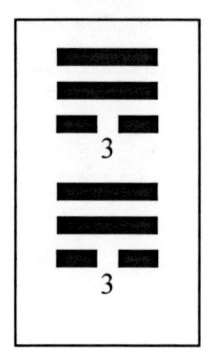

Upper and Lower trigram 3 Wind: wood, gentleness, penetration

Wind over Wind evokes; the gentle and relaxing sound of leaves rustling as the wind blows through the trees.

This hexagram represents gentleness and the eldest daughter. The clouds are penetrated by the wind which brings clarity to the world. Success will be achieved in small things only at this time.

It is advantageous to keep focused on your goal. Now is the time to plan for future action and activity. This is especially important if this move is to be a permanent one. Be patient and persistent as you steadily plod on towards your goal. The precision of your advance is more important than the speed at which it is achieved.

Don't be afraid to accept help from those wiser than yourself. Nothing useful will be achieved with brute strength and ignorance. You need strength and knowledge if you are to get anywhere with this situation.

The Hexagrams

Gentleness - Penetration (57) 033

FIRST LINE 6: Clarity and precision are what is needed now if you are to advance on your goal. This is not the time to be indecisive and undisciplined. If you are going to make a decision or promise you must adhere to it.

SECOND LINE 9: Deep rooted anger or hidden agendas lead only to confusion. This needs to be faced up to and dealt with properly before you can move on.

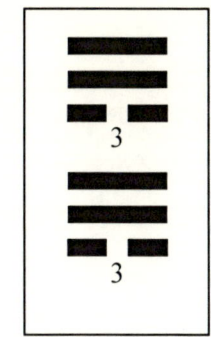

THIRD LINE 9: Come to a swift decision and don't waste time and energy worrying about possible outcomes that may never happen. Nothing good can come of this needless worry and you will be humiliated. A better use of your time would be to focus on what you wish to achieve for the future.

FOURTH LINE 6: Lively and action is more likely to lead to success in this situation. Be modest but confident toward your enemy and then you will gain satisfaction.

FIFTH LINE 9: Almost before you realize it the time is right to move. However, there is a limited window of opportunity for accomplishing your aims so make your move quickly and remain vigilant at all times.

SIXTH LINE 9: This situation has many possibilities. This is great but, don't spend too much time and energy in pondering them all. It is good to have some idea as to what is happening. However, that will do you no good if you don't have the energy left to act when the time comes.

The I Ching, the Book to turn to for Wisdom and Guidance

Endurance (32) 034

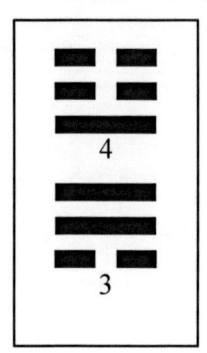

Upper trigram 4 Thunder: turbulence, awakening.

Lower trigram 3 Wind: wood, gentleness, penetration

Thunder over Wind; thunder passing quickly overhead though the wind it came in on still to blow.

This hexagram; represents the loving bond of an enduring marriage. Now is the time to stick with the original plan which works so well for you.

Slow and steady progress is called for while you fight to stay upright in the storms raging all around you. This is not the time to be obstinate about changes in your life.

Just take a moment think about what is actually happening around you. It is always possible to find a way to adapt to any situation whilst staying true to your principles. You need to find the way forward that works for you and your situation. Your principles do not have to change. The way forward lies with modifying how you are behaving as you deal with the situation.

The Hexagrams

Endurance (32) 034

FIRST LINE 6: Now is not the time to try anything new on for size. Stick with what is familiar and works for you. Don't even try to take shortcuts for there are none to be taken at this time. Be slow and meticulous in your preparations. Then you will be ready to pounce quickly when the time is right to move forward.

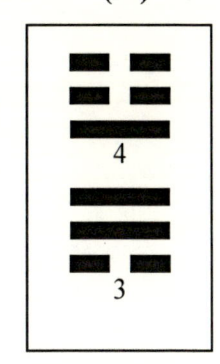

SECOND LINE 9: Whilst some movement is needed to keep things flowing in the right direction, now is not the time for a full offensive. Stay calm and wait it out.

THIRD LINE 9: You are lonely and in difficulty because you are not a nice person to be around. Your moods and emotions are extremely erratic. People are getting annoyed and frustrated with you. This is unfortunate indeed and will lead to humiliation or worse.

FOURTH LINE 9: Make sure that you know the market for whatever you are trying to sell. Do not take on goals that cannot be realistically achieved. It is better to re-evaluate what you are trying to achieve than to lose everything on a whim!

FIFTH LINE 6: Now is not the time to blindly follow tradition. Act appropriately for what you wish to achieve. The effort you put into achieving your goals must be appropriate for the goal you have in mind. Ambitious goals require boldness and innovation if you are to achieve them.

SIXTH LINE 6: Ignorance can lead to anxiety and exhaustion. This is likely to create problems for you in the future. So it is very important that you stay calm, find out what is happening and then take the right steps to deal with the situation.

The I Ching, the Book to turn to for Wisdom and Guidance

The Cauldron (50) 035

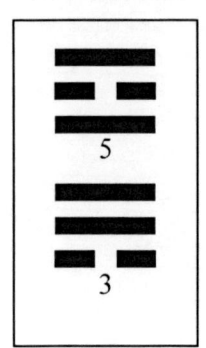

Upper trigram 5 Fire: brightness, beauty.

Lower trigram 3 Wind: wood, gentleness, penetration

Fire over Wind evokes; a hanging cooking pot over flames fanned by the rising wind, its contents will either spill or burn.

Cosmic Order – Great good fortune and progress is indicated. However, right now is not the time for taking on risky ventures. At the moment you would be better off doing ordinary things and keeping a low profile. This is the way forward to success in the present unyielding situation.

The superior man keeps the right posture and holds on firmly to what he already has.

The Hexagrams

The Cauldron (50) 035

FIRST LINE 6: If you are to achieve your goal, you will need to change how you do things, use means that would not normally be appropriate. Act with honour and sincerity to better yourself and your inexperience will not matter. Success is assured at this time.

SECOND LINE 9: Good fortune is indicated in an achievement that is of great importance to you. You set yourself apart from your fellow man to achieve your goal. Although those around you will be envious, just ignore them for it will not cause you any problems.

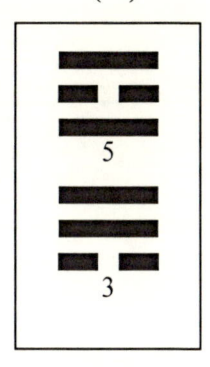

THIRD LINE 9: Although you have amazing talents, they are not being utilized because no-one realizes that you have them. This could be your own fault. Gaining a more self confident attitude about yourself will improve matters and your talents will be noticed by others. Good fortune in the end.

FOURTH LINE 9: The goals that you have set yourself are totally unrealistic. You need to be true to yourself and set achievable goals. If you do nothing to change your goals, the consequences for you and your superiors will be disastrous. The bigger goals will come in the future but for now you need to keep them manageable.

FIFTH LINE 6: The person in authority is friendly and approachable to all. He finds helpers who are both capable and willing. He must remain approachable and friendly if he is to continue forward with his goal.

SIXTH LINE 9: There is an atmosphere of greatness. The sage happily gives good advice to all who need it. Although as a result of this he finds favour with his superiors, his actions were not out of concern for his own advantage. Great good fortune results and everyone benefits here.

The I Ching, the Book to turn to for Wisdom and Guidance

Excess (28) 036

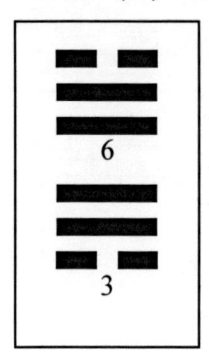

Upper trigram 6 Lake: joy, purity and truth.

Lower trigram 3 Wind: wood, gentleness, penetration

Lake over Wood evokes; a weak dam that sags and overflows drowning all in its path.

This hexagram is like a support beam that is thick in the middle but weak at the ends. The structure (your situation) is about to collapse as the weak ends of the beam collapse under the weight of those above.

Plans and foundations need to be laid before the work can commence. With plans in place you can work smarter, not harder towards your goal then there will be good fortune.

The superior man knows that it is good to have a definite goal in mind and is aware that there is a lot of work ahead of him if he is to prevent collapse. He is not afraid to work alone and will retreat if necessary. He realizes that he has made the correct decision for the circumstances.

The Hexagrams

Excess (28) 036

FIRST LINE 6: This is a very involved task so a lot of plans and preparations need to be made prior to attempting the dangerous job of lowering the heavy roof.

SECOND LINE 9: You are energised and invigorated by the young people who come to help you. Though they are modest, they share your passion and enthusiasm for the goal you have chosen.

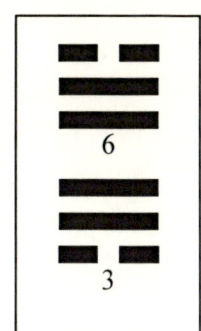

THIRD LINE 9: The ridgepole is sagging but the man keeps working on his plans, ignoring the danger. Take the advice offered by your experienced helpers. The obstacles you now face cannot be overcome with brute force and ignorance. If you try to force your way forward there will be misfortune.

FOURTH LINE 9: The ridgepole has been made safe until a permanent solution can be found. Be sincere in your actions. You have the inner strength, the ambition and drive to achieve a positive outcome in this situation. However, if you abuse your position for your own gain, you risk humiliation and public disgrace

FIFTH LINE 9: The truth has to be faced head on and steps need to be taken to make solid foundations for the future. Otherwise nothing of any use can ever be achieved.

SIXTH LINE 6: The man bravely tries to complete his task despite the enormous risks involved. He meets with misfortune but he is not to blame. Although the goal may be very important, it has a really high price tag attached to it. It would be wise to consider that before leaping into the task.

The I Ching, the Book to turn to for Wisdom and Guidance

Coming Together (44) 037

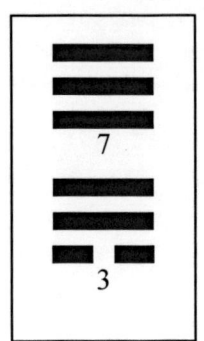

Upper trigram 7 Heaven: creative, active.

Lower trigram 3 Wind: wood, gentleness, penetration

Heaven over Wind evokes; the joyful lottery winner flying in the wind of his good fortune he surrenders to the temptations around him.

Temptation: At the time of the summer solstice, the first murmur of winter intrudes on the warmth and happiness of summer. Female goes forward to meet male. Although the sex is pleasurable, there is danger attached to it. It would be unfavourable to marry at this time.

Now is the time to rely on your own judgement and be true to yourself. You may be open to the advice of others but this is not a good time to act on it. If you do, the outcome could be most unfavourable for you.

The Hexagrams

Coming Together (44) 037

FIRST LINE 6: Now is not a good time to have a destination in mind. It is more important to deal with the immediate problem that cannot be ignored. You have the chance to stop an undesirable situation in its tracks before it can cause more problems for others. Be swift and decisive in your efforts. And all will be well.

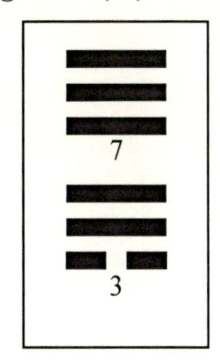

SECOND LINE 9: Keep a firm hand on any weak areas and keep them well out of sight. Things could rapidly get chaotic if others realize they exist and panic.

THIRD LINE 9: It is good to be able to push on and make a bit of extra effort as that is the path to success. However, it would be a bad mistake for you to keep going forward while your mind is not fully engaged on your task. Be absolutely certain that you know where you are and what you are doing before you make any further moves. Thus misfortune can be avoided.

FOURTH LINE 9: You are in a higher position but keeping in touch with those below you is still important. If you don't, when you find yourself in need of their input, you may find that they no longer care about your needs and ambitions. Snobbery and arrogance have no place here.

FIFTH LINE 9: The secret to success is to take good care of the people below you without them realizing that you are in control. Do this and the success and power you desire will come to you easily.

SIXTH LINE 9: Some things in life are best avoided. Be tactful when you withdraw from an inferior element and remember that it will still be there regardless. Deal with what you can before retreating quietly without making a fuss.

The I Ching, the Book to turn to for Wisdom and Guidance

The Turning point (24) 040

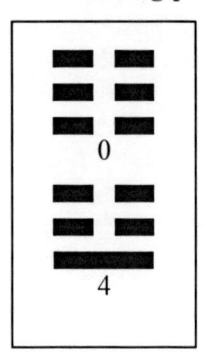

Upper trigram 0 Earth: fertility, passive.

Lower trigram 4 Thunder: turbulence, awakening.

Earth over Thunder evokes; thunder underground or perhaps the tremors before an earthquake. This is a warning, heed it and be thankful for it.

As winter solstice is the turning point of the year so you are at a turning point for change in your life. Now is the time to take seriously the old motto "off with the old and on with the new" and apply it to your life and habits. Sweep away any defunct habits, emotional debris and clutter that have held you back from living your life fully.

This will also leave room for all the good things coming your way. You are now free to move in any direction you choose.

Regarding a specific problem or situation you are currently trying to resolve, do not be afraid to go where you have never been before. Do not allow the fear of the unknown to stop you from making a move. The brave will not live forever but those who are fearful will not live at all.

Renewal and recovery are now possible because the cycle of decay is at an end. Energy and enthusiasm are returning once more to revitalize all and give rise to recovery.

The Hexagrams

The Turning point (24) 040

FIRST LINE 9: You are trying ideas on for size but they don't sit comfortably with your principles. It would be wise to apply a disciplined approach and stick with what feels right to you. You will not be blamed for your actions; in fact doing this brings you good fortune.

SECOND LINE 6: When turning back, do not be too proud to find help anywhere you can. Follow an example set by someone else and all will be well. You might ask yourself how would my Dad/ a famous actor/scout leader or someone else you admire get out of this mess and visualize following their steps out of this situation. Good fortune.

THIRD LINE 6: Make up your mind and stick to it. To constantly change your mind because you think another way may have advantages leads to nothing at all getting done. This is dangerous for you may eventually lose sight of the path. If you see the danger turn back before it is too late, the situation will eventually right itself.

FOURTH LINE 6: Although you are fed up with your current situation and wish to make changes by moving in another direction you should be aware that you may have to do so alone. Your friends may not wish to follow you. Although it is very hard to leave them behind, you must if you are to improve your life.

FIFTH LINE 6: Turning round and inspecting your own faults takes courage and strength of character. However in doing this, you will find the inner strength and the skills needed to overcome them. You will come out of this a stronger, happier person.

SIXTH LINE 6: You realize too late that change is necessary to move forward with your life. Unfortunately you will have a long wait. It is too late to turn back now and you must wait out the complete cycle before another opportunity arises.

The I Ching, the Book to turn to for Wisdom and Guidance

Nourishment (27) 041

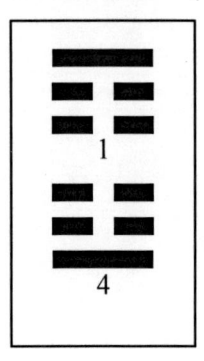

Upper trigram 1 Mountain: arresting, stillness.

Lower trigram 4 Thunder: turbulence, awakening.

Mountain over Thunder evokes; Thunderous noise then silence in mountain valleys.

In the silence, after a thunder storm (or avalanche) people focus on rescue efforts, all else is of little importance now.

Right now it is imperative that you are restrained in all your activities, mental, physical or emotional. The small stuff must not be allowed to distract you from what needs to be done now. Concentrate only on matters of real importance. All will be well if you follow this advice.

Be aware of the requirements of those around you whom you currently nourish or wish to nourish. It is vital that you remember to nourish yourself as well.

The wise man nourishes those who have talent and vision and they in turn reach out to nourish more people and so it goes on. The nourishment offered is both physical and spiritual. There will be good fortune if everyone is properly nourished.

The Hexagrams

Nourishment (27) 041

FIRST LINE 9: Be pleased for those who prosper around you whilst keeping a tight hold of your own life journey. If you let Jealousy take hold in your life, there will be great misfortune.

SECOND LINE 6: You are well able to nourish yourself and so you can be self sufficient. Yet you seek nourishment in all the wrong places. Taking food from a food bank when you can feed yourself is like stealing food from those who are hungry. Such undesirable behaviour can only lead to misfortune and disgrace.

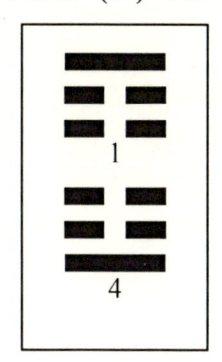

THIRD LINE 6: Seeking nourishment with no destination in mind will not nourish the body or soul. You might as well not have any nourishment at all. There is no satisfaction or resolution in this endless situation.

FOURTH LINE 6: You are no longer seeking nourishment just for yourself; you also use your position to help others in their search for nourishment. You may need to find like-minded helpers along the way but you will be successful. This is not a mistake.

FIFTH LINE 6: Now is not the time to cross the great water or take on something big. You know that others need help to gain nourishment but are not able to help them by yourself. You are not yet fully nourished and do not have enough strength. You need to get help for them from someone with the strength you lack.

SIXTH LINE 9: Now is the time to cross the great water. He is now a great sage himself and has everything he needs to nourish, educate and influence those around him who need help. He is aware of the pitfalls of this task but continues any way knowing his obligation to help. He will be successful in his endeavours and make a lot of people very happy.

The I Ching, the Book to turn to for Wisdom and Guidance

Initial Difficulties (3) 042

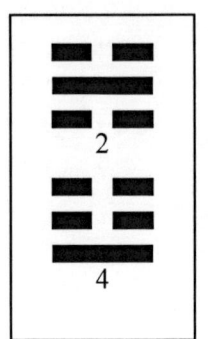

Upper trigram 2 Water: a pit, danger and chasm.

Lower trigram 4 Thunder: turbulence, awakening.

Water over Thunder evokes; tempests above and earth quakes below - cruel conditions for seeds and saplings.

A spring time shoot struggles upward through the earth but eventually pokes its head towards the sun. After a thunder storm the pent up tension is released, air is cleared and things are a lot calmer.

Despite a rocky and difficult start you will, with firm and correct action make exceptional progress towards your goal. However, do not reach too far ahead at this time.

Self reliance in this case is not a virtue so don't be afraid to ask for help from others who are knowledgeable. This help could well be what makes this project have a successful outcome. Unfortunately, however despite the storm being, over now is not a time of rest and peace.

Thunder clears the air. The superior man has the right idea when he uses his time to gain help and support from others. He knows it would be disaster to move too quickly so he waits for the right time to make his move from chaos to order.

The Hexagrams

Initial Difficulties   (3)   042

FIRST LINE 9: Across the beginning of your path lies an obstacle but you should carefully consider what you do next. Do not blunder blindly forward. The wise man humbly chooses his helpers with care.

SECOND LINE 6: Your situation is very confusing and right now you can't make any logical decisions. You would be wise to get a good night's sleep and wait for the situation to return to normal.

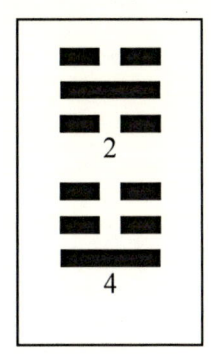

THIRD LINE 6: Do not go any further without a guide. You might not be able to physically see the difficulties ahead but you have a gut feeling that they are there. Don't ignore that gut feeling. Take some time to re-evaluate your strategies.

FOURTH LINE 6: This is a good time to move forward but if you are hesitant there will be no progress. You are unable to act alone but there is no shame in this. The situation is a difficult and dangerous one and help is needed if you are to reach your goal.

FIFTH LINE 9: Now is not the time for big undertakings. Despite being in a position of authority, you have yet to establish yourself. A calm, confident approach will work best in this situation.

SIXTH LINE 6: Unfortunately you will have to make a fresh start because you have lost your objectivity about the situation and no longer see things as they actually are. Another way forward can be found but you will have to put your mind to it.

The I Ching, the Book to turn to for Wisdom and Guidance

Increase (42) 043

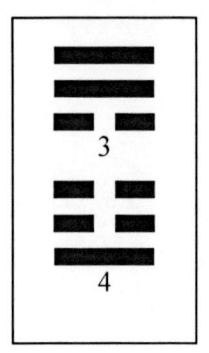

Upper trigram 3 Wind: wood, gentleness, penetration

Lower trigram 4 Thunder: turbulence, awakening.

Wood over Thunder evokes; rumbling and thunder (rapid growth in the roots) beneath a fruit tree, there could well be a bumper harvest this summer.

Penetrating growth (Wind and Thunder) forms the condition for Benefit. An enlightened person thinks about the needs of others as well as his own.

The sages who compiled the I Ching had a saying that they lived by - *"To rule is to serve"* Those above have plenty and gladly share their bounty with those below who do not have enough. The way forward is clearly visible and leads to unexpected help and good fortune. The time is right to safely cross the great water.

The superior man can see the good in others and is attracted towards it. He is also able to clearly see where he has been going wrong and changes his ways to correct this.

The Hexagrams

Increase (42) 043

FIRST LINE 9: you have an untarnished reputation. Keep it that way by undertaking a task that helps not only you but those around you. Success will be yours and you will be popular with others.

SECOND LINE 6: You are successful because you pursue worthwhile aims. This will continue if you don't make changes to the values you live by.

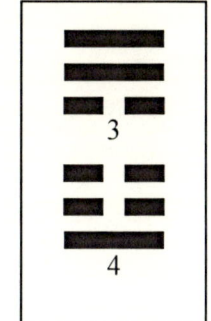

THIRD LINE 6: You are benefiting from some unfortunate circumstances. If you listen to your conscience and stay true to your principles, you will be free from reproach.

FOURTH LINE 6: You have been trusted enough to be offered the role of mediator. Your must truly have the good of the people at heart when you are giving advice. Stay calm and give advice in a way that can be understood by all. It will be put to good use. All will be well.

FIFTH LINE 9: Great good fortune comes from a kind act committed without thought of personal gain. The ruler bestows good things upon his people but asks for nothing in return.

SIXTH LINE 9: Although you are well able to help others, you choose not to. This is not a smart move. You will lose your position because people resent you for not helping them. You will be lonely and vulnerable now.

The I Ching, the Book to turn to for Wisdom and Guidance

Thunderclap (51) 044

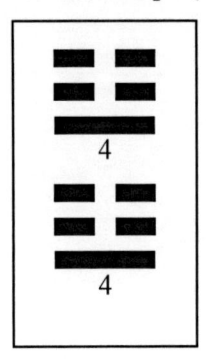

Upper and Lower trigram 4 Thunder: turbulence, awakening.

Thunder over Thunder evokes; thunder both above and below ground wow, this must be some storm!

This trigram indicates energy forcing its way upward terrifying everyone as they are caught unawares as if by an earthquake or clap of thunder.

Once everyone has calmed down and the dust has settled there will be success. Nothing important has been lost. Fear and stress is followed by joy and success.

Not all surprises will be pleasant ones. You have been badly frightened but fear is your worst enemy. When your vision and judgement are clouded by fear, problems and task seem to be much bigger than they actually are.

Let it go, take a little time to get over it and before moving again. An enlightened person carefully examines his past actions and his present life so that he may improve himself for the future.

The Hexagrams

Thunderclap (51) 044

FIRST LINE 9: You may be frightened by an unanticipated event but what you learn from it will be greatly to your advantage. Do not let the feelings generated by the fear overwhelm you. There will be relief after it is over.

SECOND LINE 6: Something really bad has happened and much has been lost. However, do not be tempted to fight fate or go looking for what you have lost. You are in more danger from the shock and your reaction to it than you are from the situation itself. Take time to breathe and re-group. Once everything has calmed down, come back and all will be well once more.

THIRD LINE 6: Your inner strength is tested by a situation outside your control. Stay calm go with the first idea that comes into your head for dealing with the situation. Although your quick action may not gain you much advantage, it will not harm you or the situation either.

FOURTH LINE 9: You are crippled by the shock this event has evoked in you. Therefore you are unprepared and can do little but wait out the situation until things have a chance to improve.

FIFTH LINE 6: Aftershocks may continue to knock you off your feet but do not go rigid with shock. You must constantly roll with them to survive. Stay fluid and change as the situation changes then you will be able to survive, keep going and accomplish something.

SIXTH LINE 6: Everyone is affected by these shocking events but you must remember that now is not the time to soldier on alone and weak. Now is not the time for action. It is far better to weather the criticism of those around you and retreat to come out again when things have calmed down.

The I Ching, the Book to turn to for Wisdom and Guidance

Biting Through   (21)   045

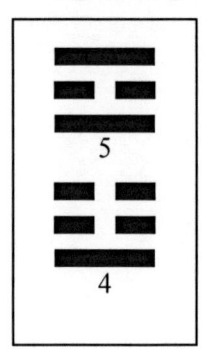

Upper trigram 5 Fire: brightness, beauty.

Lower trigram 4 Thunder: turbulence, awakening.

Fire over Thunder evokes; whenever thunder booms lightning inevitably strikes.

This hexagram resembles a mouth with the teeth biting through something. So a mouth bites through and clears the remaining obstacles that have been keeping you at a distance from your goal.

Your freedom of movement has been impeded until now by the obstacles in your path. This is the time to face up to what must be done to remove the obstacles from the path to your goal.

Your actions need to be decisive but cautious .Good fortune, problems dealt with. Now is an advantageous time to seek justice.

Thunder and lightning initiate reform. Rulers of old made their laws carefully with the penalties tailored to fit the crime committed.

The superior man is quick to take appropriate measures when someone disrupts social harmony. When handing out punishment he is clear and precise in what he does but at the same time shows compassion. In this, he earns the respect of those around him.

The Hexagrams
Biting Through (21) 045

FIRST LINE 9: This is your first offence so the punishment will be small in hopes that the shock of being punished will stop you from re-offending in the future. You can be sure that the punishment fits the crime.

SECOND LINE 6: He did not learn his lesson and continues to offend so the punishment is more severe this time. Some might argue that it is too severe but the desired purpose is achieved and he reforms his ways. There is no error in judgement here.

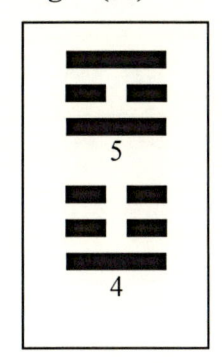

THIRD LINE 6: You had good intentions for necessary reform but you did not have the clout and power behind you to make it happen. Your efforts were ignored by some and treated with derision by others. You will recover, your actions were necessary for the good of all.

FOURTH LINE 9: You will come out of this a stronger and wiser person. From adversity comes strength and wisdom. The task you face is a hard one with a really difficult beginning but if you stand firm, stay alert and keep going, a just conclusion will eventually be reached.

FIFTH LINE 6: The judge must make a decision and stay true to it. His judgement will be just because he is continually alert to the dangers and consequences of a bad judgement.

SIXTH LINE 9: He is not learning any lessons from his punishment. He continues to stray from the path and ignores the warnings of those around him. Misfortune, the punishment this time will be severe.

The I Ching, the Book to turn to for Wisdom and Guidance

Following - Allegiance   (17)   046

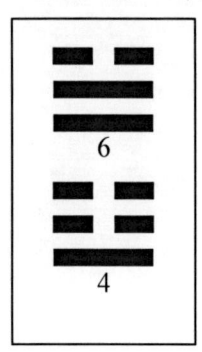

Upper trigram 6 Lake: joy, purity and truth.

Lower trigram 4 Thunder: turbulence, awakening.

Lake over Thunder evokes; thunder beneath the lake causing many ripples on the surface.

No leader should ask anyone to follow him unless he is certain that he follows the correct path.

It is indicated that you will be successful and move forward if you are adaptable and persistent with the situation at hand.

The superior man understands that he needs to recover and so turns in on himself to relax. If he resists this time of rest, he wastes valuable energy and nothing productive will have been achieved to change a bad situation.

The Hexagrams

Following - Allegiance (17) 046

FIRST LINE 9: Your goal has changed but if you persevere, there will be good fortune. It is good to go seek advice from people with a wide variety of opinions on the matter at hand. However, stick to your principles, be discerning about any advice you receive.

SECOND LINE 6: It is time to examine your goals. If they are unworthy, you run the risk of losing all that you have worked towards so far. Perhaps you should consider changing them to something more appropriate.

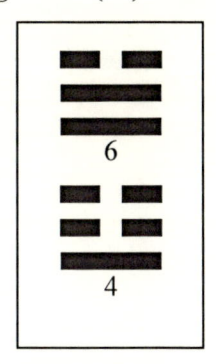

THIRD LINE 6: You are letting go of all the old and out of date parts of your life and are moving on to something more in tune with situation you find yourself in. You will find that a brighter future awaits you.

FOURTH LINE 9: There is an ulterior motive behind the allegiance of some who support you. To avoid future misfortune and loss, the path must be cleared of those self serving flatterers. Only those who are loyal and sincere should be allowed to continue with you on your path.

FIFTH LINE 9: You know in your heart what is right. Aim high and only accept the best! Be sincere and stand your ground trusting that good fortune will follow.

SIXTH LINE 6: The wise and revered sage is asked to guide one of his followers. There will be some personal involvement with that person. If he teaches sincerely he will be rewarded for his unselfishness toward another.

The I Ching, the Book to turn to for Wisdom and Guidance

Innocence (25) 047

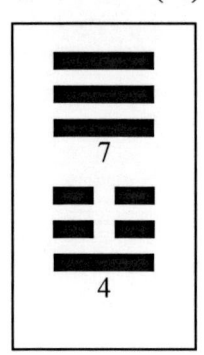

Upper trigram 7 Heaven: creative, active.

Lower trigram 4 Thunder: turbulence, awakening.

Earth over Thunder; the dragon flies high to avoid the thunder raging below.

Innocence as in the purity of a virgin landscape untouched by a developer not the innocence of the naïve. This is a good time to tune into your inner self and to be true to what you find there. What are your true desires in life? Make an effort to find out and act on them then there will be good fortune.

The reverse is also true; if you shove aside your own desires while helping others to satisfy theirs, you will be the one who is unhappy and frustrated. Life is not a rehearsal so if you are to succeed in life, you need to put yourself first and choose to participate in what life has to offer. You can still help others but you must do so on your own terms.

When misfortune comes to one who is innocent by nature, the consequences will not be very serious and they will pass quickly, without major incident.

The Hexagrams

Innocence   (25)   047

FIRST LINE 9: This is the time to act instinctively trusting in your gut feeling and what you know to be right. Devious or selfish action may lead to success but that is short lived as in the end you will fail.

SECOND LINE 6: Everything has its appointed time and sequence for completion. If you wish to be successful in your current endeavours, you must keep your mind firmly focused on what you are doing right now. This is not the time to day dream about achieving your future desires.

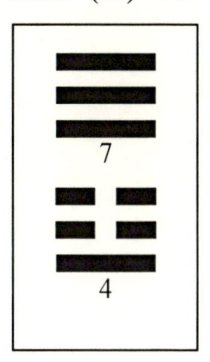

THIRD LINE 6: Although you are going through a time of unexpected misfortune, you should remain calm and avoid being careless. If you do not lock up your bicycle, you cannot assume that it will still be there when you come back for it. Innocent faith in the honesty of others is misplaced and you are the loser here.

FOURTH LINE 9: Stay true to and have trust in your inmost thoughts and ideas, do not be influenced or distracted by outside influences. Do this and you will be free from error.

FIFTH LINE 9: Although you are ill, now is not the time to rely on medicine or a Doctor. The solution to your problem will come in its own time. You must let nature take its course.

SIXTH LINE 9: Now is not the time to try anything new or different to what you are accustomed to. This is a favourable time for those who have no plans or destination in mind. Don't do anything at all, just patiently wait it out. If you insist on recklessly pushing on now, you will fail miserably.

The I Ching, the Book to turn to for Wisdom and Guidance

Sinking Light (36) 050

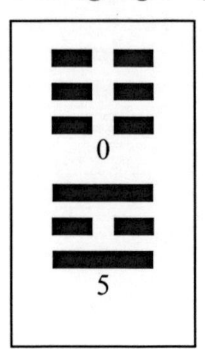

Upper trigram 0 Earth: fertility, passive.

Lower trigram 5 Fire: brightness, beauty.

Earth over Fire; earth puts out the fire extinguishing its warmth and light in the process.

In this time a sinking light, correct persistence is advantageous. Do not allow yourself to become depressed by the difficult and gloomy situation you find yourself in.

This is a good time to blend in with the crowd whilst allowing your inner self to shine out through the darkness. Right now you must trust in yourself and rely on your inner strength carry you through this tough situation.

It is important when darkness is all around to get an idea of the true severity of the situation you are in. This will help you focus and guide you forward.

The superior man understands that shining a light in the darkness will not make much difference here. If necessary he will remove himself from the situation to re-group to save his energies.

Showing due respect and consideration towards yourself and others is always relevant and important whatever the situation. Your persistence will be rewarded.

Remember, the sun may indeed have set but the light will return anew the next day, it is not gone forever!

Sinking Light (36) 050

FIRST LINE 9: Now is not the time to pay attention to small matters. If you do, you will not have the strength to overcome the obstacles that lie ahead of you. Although you may need to retreat from these obstacles, persistence toward your true goal will be honoured and rewarded in the end. Others may be very critical of your persistence but you need to ignore them and keep going.

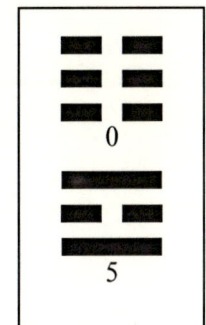

SECOND LINE 6: You have been injured in the line of duty. How you cope with that injury and keep going toward your goal will make you a role model for others in a similar position. You still manage to assist those in need of your help. Which is after all your main reason for soldiering on?

THIRD LINE 9: Although you are in a position to grab control of the situation, now is not time to rock the boat with a lot of changes. Although these changes are necessary they cannot be made all at once. To try would be to recklessly risk all for nothing.

FOURTH LINE 6: You are in a good position to get a clear view of exactly you are up against in this situation. If it seems dangerous then now is most likely a good time to back off and retreat from the situation.

FIFTH LINE 6: Although you are an important player in this situation you must hide your actual thoughts and feelings on the situation and go with the flow. This is not the time to struggle against and resist what is happening around you. If you do not struggle you will be rewarded in the end. However, do not forget your actual thoughts just wait it out for now and strike when the time is right.

SIXTH LINE 6: The darkness will ultimately destroy itself and those who were in control will be consigned to distant nightmares. Good will prevail.

The I Ching, the Book to turn to for Wisdom and Guidance

Grace (22) 051

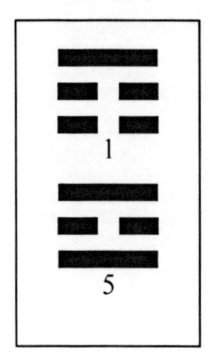

Upper trigram 1 Mountain: arresting, stillness.

Lower trigram 5 Fire: brightness, beauty.

Mountain over Fire evokes; fire in the valley does not reach up to light up the mountain above it.

There is fire below the mountain, the symbol of grace. In small matters it is advantageous to focus on a goal and go forward with it.

Be calm when dealing with the inner workings of any organization you are dealing with. If petty disputes should arise, they must not be allowed to distract you from your goal. It is important at this time that you understand the rules and follow them very carefully.

This is a good time to improve your image but do so without fuss. Make sure that you are aware of what is expected and behave accordingly.

The Hexagrams

Grace (22) 051

FIRST LINE 9: The wise man takes good care of himself as he moves upward from the subordinate position he once held. He learns that in order to progress forward, he must work hard, taking no shortcuts or half measures.

SECOND LINE 6: Although the vessel is beautiful to behold, do not allow your admiration to blind you to what is inside it. If you do, you risk missing its true meaning. Sometimes what is in the vessel is more important than what it looks like.

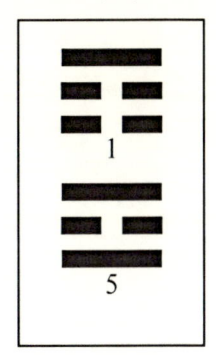

THIRD LINE 9: All your hard work has paid off and you are enjoying a period of good fortune. However if wish things to stay this good for any length of time you must keep up your efforts.

FOURTH LINE 6: You have to choose between two paths; one path is ornate and all about how things look from the outside. This is a very shallow and narrow minded perspective of the world. Follow this and it would likely lead to misery and despair in the end. The other path involves keeping things simple and glowing from the inside. This path leads to greater self awareness/knowledge and the formation of meaningful relationships with those around you. Good fortune arises from the second path.

FIFTH LINE 6: You may not have much to offer but your sincerity will be noticed and that is what truly matters. You will eventually be recognized not for what you have to give but for who you truly are. Good fortune.

SIXTH LINE 9: Be sincere and keep things simple then there can be no misunderstandings.

The I Ching, the Book to turn to for Wisdom and Guidance

After Completion (63) 052

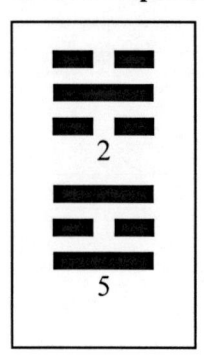

Upper trigram 2 Water: a pit, danger and chasm.

Lower trigram 5 Fire: brightness, beauty.

Water over Fire evokes; in preparation for feasting and merriment, a cauldron boils on the fire.

This hexagram is about the time after some success. It is a time to rejoice but also a time to prepare to sustain the success.

This may be a very favourable hexagram but you cannot afford to relax. It would be wise to move carefully. Although there is currently a state of balance and harmony any sudden moves could tip the scales toward the return of disorder. In the beginning there will be good fortune in small matters.

The superior man makes sure that he has a back-up plan in the event of the return of disorder.

The Hexagrams

After Completion (63) 052

FIRST LINE 9: The fox that gets his tail wet after safely crossing the water. Stress builds as your ideas move forward. You begin to doubt yourself. However, you will not allow yourself to be swept away on the wave of enthusiasm. You will not be adversely affected by what you have begun because on the whole your thoughts are correct.

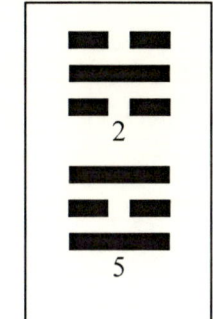

SECOND LINE 6: Despite being vulnerable, now is the time to do nothing but patiently sit things out. Taking action now brings misfortune. Recognition is coming and the situation will right itself soon enough.

THIRD LINE 9: Despite a long, hard struggle, it is possible now to achieve your dream. Make sure that any people taken on to assist in this endeavour are skilled and knowledgeable in their work.

FOURTH LINE 6: The problem or situation about which you enquire shows evidence of decay. Know that everything deteriorates eventually. It is important now to take the right precautions. Keep your eyes open and your guard up at all times to avoid misfortune.

FIFTH LINE 9: This is the time to be sincere in all you do and take things in small steps. You can achieve a lot this way. However, if you try to show off lavishly boasting about your successes, you will not achieve much at all. It is not the size of the offering but the sincerity with which it is offered that really matters here.

SIXTH LINE 6: Do not look back after a successful escape! Keep going forward, looking only in the direction you are heading. Shirking the responsibilities that come with the action you have started will lead to danger and misfortune.

The I Ching, the Book to turn to for Wisdom and Guidance

The Family (37)   053

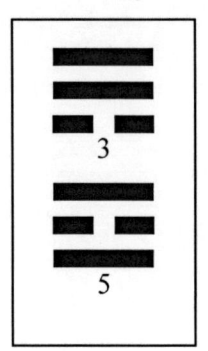

Upper trigram 3 Wind: wood, gentleness, penetration

Lower trigram 5 Fire: brightness, beauty.

Wood over Fire evokes; a fire burning brightly in a hut bringing warmth, comfort and security to the occupants.

This hexagram symbolizes family and all that comes with it. Loyalty, a firm hand and strong leadership are called for at this time if you are to succeed in your goal.

It is important that you know your place both in family and in society and behave appropriately.

For your own peace of mind, obligations have to be met and promises kept no matter how hard that task may be.

Respect and caring for others is deemed important in every family. This should be applied to all other areas of your life as well e.g. co-workers in an office, class mates at school.

The Hexagrams

The Family (37) 053

FIRST LINE 9: If all is to go well in a relationship, your expectations need to be clearly defined. A child needs loving kindness and firmness to grow up with discipline. If the parents do not instil this message from the first, they will have cause to regret it in when the child they are raising is out of control.

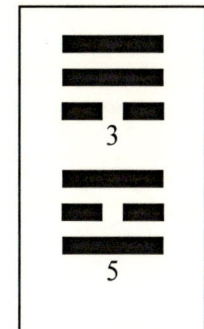

SECOND LINE 6: Now is not the time to follow your own desires for there is a lot to be done for the household. There will be good fortune if the needs of all in the community are met.

THIRD LINE 9: Keep a tight rein on your temper and remain calm as you try to find a solution to the quarrels within the family. Calmness and order must prevail in order to avoid chaos. Discipline and tenderness are the best tools for the job in hand.

FOURTH LINE 6: A woman in the family (could be a Daughter or Daughter-in-Law) works hard to maintain the health and well being of the family. There is great good fortune.

FIFTH LINE 9: The people do not fear their leader (Head of the household, perhaps the Father) because he is kind and treats them fairly. This kind of relationship leads to good fortune for everyone.

SIXTH LINE 9: You have are a very caring person with a good sense of ethics and responsibility towards others. This makes you a respected member of society. There will be good fortune to you and your dependents. People come to you for advice.

The I Ching, the Book to turn to for Wisdom and Guidance

Abundance (55) 054

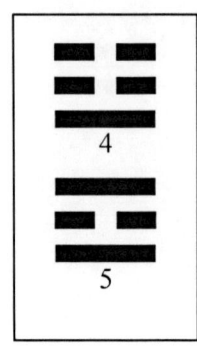

Upper trigram 4 Thunder: turbulence, awakening.

Lower trigram 5 Fire: brightness, beauty.

Thunder over Fire evokes; thunder during the day. The sky clouds and sky are dark but the lightning lights up the fields of golden corn below.

Like the sun at midday, its highest point, this wonderfully abundant situation cannot remain so forever. Now is the time to make the most of the situation and move forward while you can. This is a time of great happiness and good fortune, ideas come to fruition.

Now is not the time to be worrying about what might happen in the future. Enjoy the now, be happy with what you have and all will be well.

Abundance (55) 054

FIRST LINE 9: While working on this project, friendship with one who is like-minded blossoms. Working together brings clarity and enthusiasm to the project. This is good for everyone and should be encouraged. Sadly, this situation is not permanent and there will come a time of restlessness and a desire to get moving again. Take heed of this and all will be well.

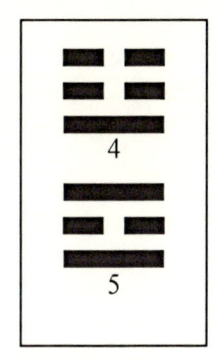

SECOND LINE 6: Be sincere and honest but do not attempt to forge heedlessly ahead. There are obstacles in your path that are not your fault. To move forward now would invite the envy and hatred of those around you. It is important that you remain loyal to your principles and beliefs. Be patient and sit this out until the time is right. Remember that there will be good fortune in the end.

THIRD LINE 9: The bungling and ineptitude are at their zenith but will not remain so forever. This is the time to wait patiently for things to improve - as the sun at its zenith eventually wanes so shall this situation. There will be no blame.

FOURTH LINE 9: Your grim situation is about to be reversed. It is nearly time to act. You will finally get to work with the right people to get you out of this rut and move forward. Intelligent decisions and enthusiasm for the project will lead you steadily into good fortune.

FIFTH LINE 6: Be modest in your endeavours and ask for help from those who are knowledgeable. There will be great good fortune and rewards everyone concerned.

SIXTH LINE 6: Your single minded pursuit of material gain has made you proud and isolated. Your pride has cost you dearly! You have lost your most precious treasure of all, the friendship and love of those who were closest to you. Things will never hug you back!

The I Ching, the Book to turn to for Wisdom and Guidance

The fire of knowledge   (30)   055

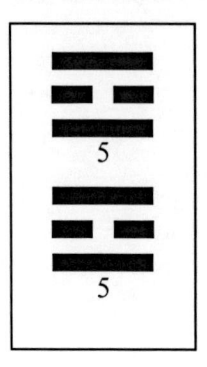

Upper and Lower trigram 5 Fire: brightness, beauty.

Fire over Fire evokes; the light and warmth of a fire as it burns brightly through the night casting its rosy glow on everything around it.

We all have limitations in one form or another. For your personal freedom and development, now is the time to see them. You also have to understand that no-one is perfect and not everything can be achieved in this world.

The superior man knows that intelligence lights the way forward when it is properly nurtured. Like a teacher nurturing the intelligence of his students.

Persistence is advantageous just now and with it comes good fortune. If you understand the facts of the situation you will be calmer and the solution will be more effective.

The fire of knowledge   (30)   055

FIRST LINE 9: When starting out on a new path or venture do not allow first impressions to overwhelm and confuse your mind. Take a deep breath, remain calm and focus on the goal ahead as you move cautiously forward.

SECOND LINE 6: The sun is fully up to light the way. This is a time of great good fortune. Be cautious of lofty goals and over-engineering the situation. Keep it simple and take the middle path then all will be well.

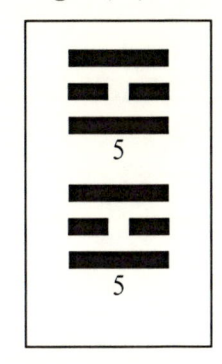

THIRD LINE 9: Smile as you enjoy the beautiful colours of the setting sun. Remember fondly what has gone before and relish the thought of what is yet to come. This is not a time to sadly dwell on what is past and shudder at the thought of what the future may hold. Such sadness will only become an obstacle to your freedom.

FOURTH LINE 9: There is no such thing as overnight success. True and sustained success comes slowly with lots of hard work. Sudden and unexpected success is very intense but lasts only for a short time then dies away quickly as no-one has the energy to keep that pace going indefinitely.

FIFTH LINE 6: This is a time of great change, upheaval and letting go of the past. There may be grief and sadness but it is still a time of good fortune. This will ultimately be a change for the better for all concerned.

SIXTH LINE 9: It is your job to find the source of the problem and remove it. You must be very careful how you do it. Your thoughts may have been muddled by others who have not been honest with you about the situation you face. If you are successful in getting rid of the root of this situation, order will restore itself and things will calm down.

The I Ching, the Book to turn to for Wisdom and Guidance

Tempered Revolution   (49)   056

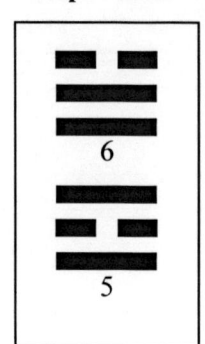

Upper trigram 6 Lake: joy, purity and truth.

Lower trigram 5 Fire: brightness, beauty.

Lake over Fire; when the underwater volcano erupts upward in fire, the waters of the lake will be vaporised.

The wise man sees the coming revolution but waits until the time is right before joining the fray.

This is not the time to struggle against change. This is an excellent chance for you to come to terms with your past, both the good and the bad. Then you will be unencumbered as the much needed changes are put into action.

The world all around you is undergoing rapid changes. If you wish to move forward and be a part of this, you must become more adaptable and embrace the changes.

Although the changes will seem a little daunting while in progress once they have been achieved, confidence will soar and there will be great progress. It is time to remember that you are a survivor, not a victim!

The Hexagrams

Tempered Revolution (49) 056

FIRST LINE 9: You must keep a close eye on the situation. Wait until you are certain that the time is right before you leap into the action.

SECOND LINE 6: A critical time has come where change is essential and timing is everything. If the change is to be successful, you must have the right attitude while remaining focused on the end result. If you have all this and the support of those around you, you will be very successful in what you achieve.

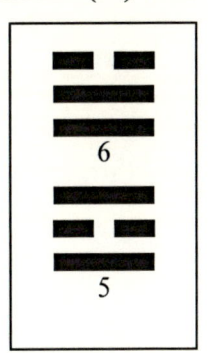

THIRD LINE 9: Quick and thoughtless action now would court disaster. Take the time to carefully assess the situation before making the changes. Once you are certain what is involved and what its effects are likely to be, go forward in a carefully planned manner.

FOURTH LINE 9: Great change is happening. If your preparations are in place there will be good fortune if you have sound reasons for going ahead. The results should be worthy of all the effort you are putting in.

FIFTH LINE 9: You are in the right position to bring about meaningful change to the situation. You have the vision and determination to bring it about. This is the time to trust yourself and your gut feelings on this and go with them.

SIXTH LINE 6: The changes have been implemented and now it is time to wrangle out the small details. Striving for perfection will only lead to discord. Instead, be happy with what has already been achieved. Enjoy thinking about what implementing these changes means for the future. Take the middle ground and with persistence there will be good fortune.

The I Ching, the Book to turn to for Wisdom and Guidance

Companionship (13) 057

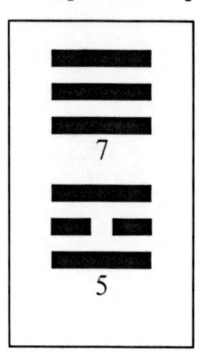

Upper trigram 7 Heaven: creative, active.

Lower trigram 5 Fire: brightness, beauty.

Heaven over Fire evokes; a traveller given a warm welcome by his companions.

This is the companionship of a strong community or a hard-working team for example firefighters.

The superior man puts aside his ego and pride. He thinks as part of a community and shows concern and consideration for the wellbeing of those around him. Progress will be made.

Companionship plays an important role in any community but a group of like minded people must be well organized if they are to flourish. If there is none, the community will be thrown into chaos.

Strength and endurance are needed now. The time is right to cross the great water. You also need to make decisions that have to be made for the good of all. Keep going and all will be well.

Clarity is very important just now because if everyone understands the situation it will be easier to strengthen and organize the whole community.

The Hexagrams

Companionship (13) 057

FIRST LINE 9: Things are out in the open now and friends who think alike and share goals can discuss the way forward as a group. Be aware, that there will be a parting of the ways as ideas change and thoughts no longer jibe together.

SECOND LINE 6: Sadly, snobbery has crept into the community straining relations for all. Power struggles and fighting break out. This can only lead to failure and disgrace as the community heads down a slippery slope.

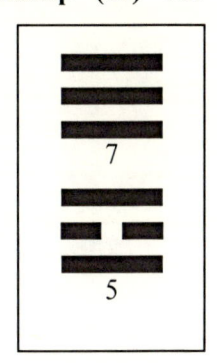

THIRD LINE 9: The community grinds to a halt due to mistrust and the selfish, self serving goals of its members. There can be no progress until hostilities cease and trust are restored to the members.

FOURTH LINE 9: You are lonely because pursuit of your dream has become more important to you than your community. You will soon come to your senses and reality will eventually return. For this to happen, you must hold out the hand of friendship once more to the community members. Then there will be good fortune for all.

FIFTH LINE 9: Show your feelings about the obstacles around you and share them with those around you. This will spur all to unify and work together to overcome them. There will be many role models formed and much happiness for the community.

SIXTH LINE 9: It is better to conduct a relationship over distance than to not have one at all. It is not a mistake to trust one another or to hope for happiness and fulfilment in the future. Your example gives others in the community hope and inspiration this is very important. Surely this is a time to pat yourself on the back, not reproach yourself?

The I Ching, the Book to turn to for Wisdom and Guidance

Approaching (19) 060

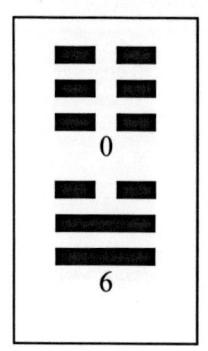

Upper trigram 0 Earth: fertility, passive.

Lower trigram 6 Lake: joy, purity and truth.

Earth over Lake; the extremely fertile plains above the lake are a blessing to all.

The superior man reaches out the ordinary folk below him. He is willing to teach and guide them. He gives supports and encourages them in their efforts to learn from him. Persistence is advantageous at this time. Great progress and success are indicated but in the eighth month there will be misfortune.

Like the beginning of spring, all is stirring and awakening. This includes forces for good and evil. Now is the time to stamp out the negative forces before their bad influence gets in the way of your goals.

Good fortune should be allowed to come of its own accord and run its course. Summer is coming but so is autumn, the natural time for decay. Move forward while you can and make the best of all the opportunities that may come your way.

Misfortune is averted when the danger is met head on before its threat becomes reality.

The Hexagrams

Approaching (19) 060

FIRST LINE 9: This is a time of good, like minded people working together in harmony. However you must make certain that your goals are worthwhile. Remain true to your principles then there will be good fortune.

SECOND LINE 9: The future is looking great on a material level. Your suggestions are getting noticed from supportive people higher up the ladder. Allowances need to be made for any obstacles that crop up along the way.

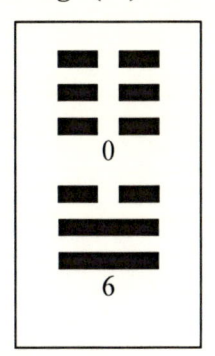

THIRD LINE 6: The promotion is coming too easily and is not fully appreciated. You are getting careless and that is dangerous for the future. It is not too late to reverse this trend. If you pull back and notice what you are doing, mistakes can be avoided. Quick action now will save the day.

FOURTH LINE 6: You gain promotion but you stay alert. Your behaviour is still right for any situation you may encounter. This brings good fortune and success. The powerful superior takes the newly promoted under his wing and into his circle. This helps him continue moving positively forward.

FIFTH LINE 6: You are in a powerful role of leadership and must choose your helpers and advisors with great care. If you are to win their respect, you will need to trust them and their skills enough to leave them to get the job done. This shows that you respect their abilities then you will win their respect for not interfering.

SIXTH LINE 6: Having reached a position of great authority, he gladly shares his wisdom and experience with others. This brings great progress and good fortune to all concerned. It is also the sign of a great leader.

The I Ching, the Book to turn to for Wisdom and Guidance

Decrease (41) 061

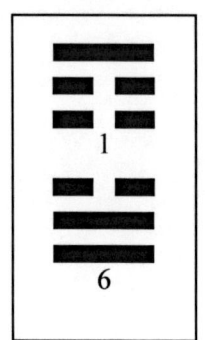

Upper trigram 1 Mountain: arresting, stillness.

Lower trigram 6 Lake: joy, purity and truth.

Mountain over Lake; the mountain replenishes the lake below it each summer as the melting snow on the peaks sends waters downward.

Now is the time for restraint and prudence in everything you do. There is no place for your anger and indignation. Be very careful what you say or do.

If you are to survive in this time of adversity, you should use your inner strength to work out how to simplify and organize your life. It is good to have a destination in mind and make a sincere and determined effort to reach it. If you do all of this, good fortune will follow soon.

If you are not sure how to proceed consult a wise expert but make sure that you are sincere and respectful when you do so. It is not the size of the offering that matters but how sincerely it is offered.

The Hexagrams

Decrease (41) 061

FIRST LINE 9: Get your own work done before you offer to help another. Think carefully before you do so. Know how much burden you can carry and how much responsibility you are willing to take on before you offer to help.

SECOND LINE 9: Your principles must never be sacrificed to help another. You should not be diminished as you replenish others. This is not a worthwhile exercise.

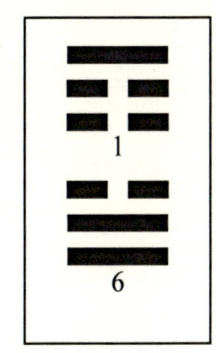

THIRD LINE 6: Working in threes simply does not work. If three start a job, one will get lost along the way. However, if one begins alone, he will not always remain so.

FOURTH LINE 6: As you make the effort to face up to your shortcomings and do something about them, others will come forward to help you. Humble gratitude toward those who help will help you brings joy to all.

FIFTH LINE 6: The omens are favourable. There is nothing to fear, nothing getting in the way of your good fortune and future happiness. Go for it and enjoy all that comes your way.

SIXTH LINE 9: You have risen to a higher position whilst doing no harm to others. This is of great benefit to all. You honestly gained your position through persistence and hard work. Your efforts are now devoted to the good of all. There is no error.

The I Ching, the Book to turn to for Wisdom and Guidance

Restraint (60) 062

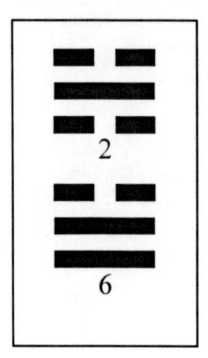

Upper trigram 2 Water: a pit, danger and chasm.

Lower trigram 6 Lake: joy, purity and truth.

Water over Lake; the lake is unable to spread itself because it is contained within a deep chasm.

At the moment your life is very limited. No matter how hard you try, it is just not possible to have everything you want right now. These limitations have been imposed to curb expenditure and so forth. If they are appropriate, there will be progress in the right direction. However, if they are excessively harsh, that is will only cause rebellion and serve no purpose.

The Hexagrams

Restraint (60) 062

FIRST LINE 9: This is not the right time to follow your aims. Don't waste your energies trying to overcome the visible obstacles ahead. Instead, conserve your energies to be ready for a decisive move when the time is right.

SECOND LINE 9: Too much limitation now could cost you the chance to move when the time is right. Immediate and unhindered action at the right moment is vital if you are to make any progress.

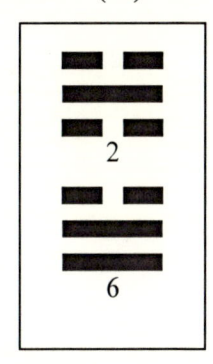

THIRD LINE 6: You are the victim of your own past extravagances. If you keep making the same mistakes now, you will have cause for regret. In order to avoid further problems in the future; you will need to learn from your past mistakes and take responsibility for your own actions.

FOURTH LINE 6: These limitations need to become an instinctive part of your life. Do not bear grudges or hide your head in a bucket. Be flexible and take responsible steps to rectify the situation immediately then continue on your way. This will lead you to a successful future.

FIFTH LINE 6: Be modest and become a role model for others to follow as you deal with your own problems responsibly. Going forward brings good fortune. Allowing others to learn something from how you deal with your situation is a valuable gift for all.

SIXTH LINE 6: Being ruthless toward yourself may well be what saves you from this self inflicted situation. However you should not try to impose unfair and excessive restrictions on those around you. All you will achieve is feeling their frustration and resentment as they vent it at you, the cause of their unhappiness. However, remember that over time resentment dissipates and life goes on.

The I Ching, the Book to turn to for Wisdom and Guidance

Inner Truth   (61)   063

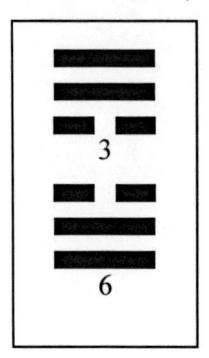

Upper trigram 3 Wind: wood, gentleness, penetration

Lower trigram 6 Lake: joy, purity and truth.

Wind over Lake; wind is perfumed by the fresh scents coming off the lake.

This is a time for careful negotiation and the moderation of rigid ideas.

You are working with all kinds of people right now and not all of them are able to communicate as well as you do. Be respectful, keep smiling and keep your message simple for all to absorb.

You need to explain things carefully every step of the way. It will be repeated many times before everyone understands but in the end it will be worthwhile. You will also have to be patient and not lose your temper with these people, no matter how dim witted they seem.

It is advantageous to cross the great water. Good fortune.

The Hexagrams

Inner Truth (61)

FIRST LINE 9: Look inside yourself for guidance in this matter. Rely on your own judgement and true nature. If you look elsewhere for answers, you will likely be sucked into the chaos and disorientation that is all around you. Dealing with things your way brings good fortune.

SECOND LINE 9: How you are in your actions and communications to others shows the kind of person you are. You rally the hearts and minds of the people around you boosting their morale. Their response will be warm and favourable towards you. Good fortune.

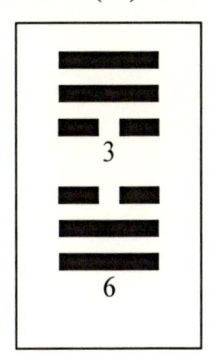

THIRD LINE 6: A time of emotional upheaval, and hesitancy, a time of flagging self confidence. You are not at all sure how you should proceed with this thorny problem. Do you reveal the truth or do you withhold it for the good of all? The answers must be sought from outside yourself this time as you are not steady enough to provide them from within yourself. The answer is shrouded in cloud.

FOURTH LINE 6: You seek enlightenment and a goal that is bigger than you are. It is important for the sake of your inner confidence that you ask questions and find out what makes it so powerful. In this way you can gain the inner confidence needed to help those you left behind.

FIFTH LINE 9: Others are drawn to the ruler's side calmed and reassured by the good vibes that come from him. The ruler helps and guides the people forward with his inner strength and courage.

SIXTH LINE 9: Although you may be able to ask for help to reach your goal, now is not a good time for you to act. Be patient and wait it out. Persist with your plans and there will only be despair.

The I Ching, the Book to turn to for Wisdom and Guidance

The Marrying Maiden   (54)   064

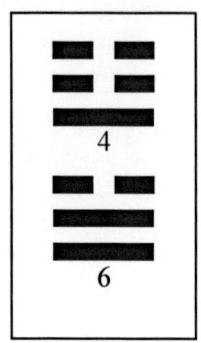

Upper trigram 4 Thunder: turbulence, awakening.

Lower trigram 6 Lake: joy, purity and truth.

Thunder over Lake evokes; thunder high in the air that causes the lake surface to tremble but the lake is not able to rise and follow the thunder.

An older man marries a much younger woman. She is his second wife and this is deemed to be a good omen for the future. This marriage is symbolic and should not be taken literally to mean a marriage; it could just as easily be any situation you are dealing with.

Sadly, the young woman does not behave appropriately for her new position in life. She has not considered the perils and pitfalls of her situation before making her move. This is a bad mistake to make and does not bode well for her future.

Don't even think about making a move in any direction. Keep your head down and make sure that your behaviour offends no-one. Work hard to maintain good relations with everyone you deal with at home or professionally. Don't leave yourself open to any form of criticism. This is not the time to risk anything on new ventures or gambling.

Think about how your problem looks in the distant future and ask yourself what you can do to stop the situation getting any worse.

The Hexagrams

The Marrying Maiden (54) 064

FIRST LINE 9: You may not have power or high status but you have earned the protection and trust of someone who is of high status. Be tactful and diplomatic to influence the situation for the mutual good of both of you.

SECOND LINE 9: The situation is not at all what you were expecting. You have been left with the task of carrying on the dream. Your Sense of purpose and devotion to the cause will eventually be recognized and bring a successful outcome.

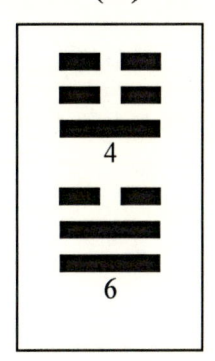

THIRD LINE 6: The first chance for success that comes your way will only bring a small advance. You will have to compromise and be prepared to make sacrifices if you are to achieve anything positive.

FOURTH LINE 9: This is the time to watch the world go by as you wait for a more opportune time to make your move. Your motives were correct and your patience will be rewarded soon.

FIFTH LINE 6: You may have high status and wealth but you will not accomplish much until you can let go of your pride. You must be prepared to ignore your social position to help others less fortunate than you are. This will bring good fortune.

SIXTH LINE 6: You are not sincere in your actions. Like a wooden puppet you do the "right thing" out of a false sense of obligation and duty. Someone else pulls your strings. No destination is favourable and there is no advantage in moving any further along this path.

The I Ching, the Book to turn to for Wisdom and Guidance

Opposites (38) 065

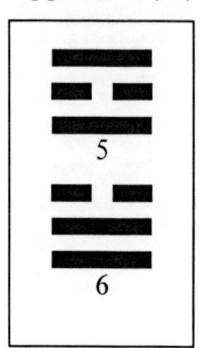

Upper trigram 5 Fire: brightness, beauty.

Lower trigram 6 Lake: joy, purity and truth.

Fire over Lake; it does not seem possible to set a lake on fire yet as the sun sets over the lake its waters seem to flicker and glow orange and yellow as if on fire.

This is a time opposites and of good fortune in small things.

The second daughter and the youngest daughter live under the same roof. They are siblings but have totally different personalities. They each need be their own person yet respect one another's point of view; this is not easy!

In your situation, the views of others slow down your progress. They do not wish you any harm; they just have a different opinion to yours. This is where you need to agree to differ and work on a compromise that will make everyone happy.

The Hexagrams

Opposites (38) 065

FIRST LINE 9: Forcing the two parties to shake hands and work together again will not work. The situation will have to be lived with until over time the issues amicably resolve themselves. You need to stay calm and positive if you are to avoid future mistakes.

SECOND LINE 9: An accidental meeting of people not on speaking terms in a narrow street leads to friendly overtures. They can't avoid one another so politeness forces them to be friendly. The dispute is resolved through calm discussion perhaps over a coffee. This meeting is no accident and should not be considered a mistake. Natural attraction is playing its part in this.

THIRD LINE 6: Despite numerous problems and blocked turnings, there will be a happy ending to all this. Have faith and hold on firmly to what you know to be right.

FOURTH LINE 9: You have been shunned by the community for your opposing views. Luckily you meet someone who shares your views and is willing to team up with you to resolve the situation. Working with this person, you can make a better future for both of you. Keep your guard up until you are sure where you stand.

FIFTH LINE 6: He is focused on keeping safe in a bad situation and does not see or recognize an old friend genuinely who wants to help. Your friend is not insulted because he understands the situation you are in. He comes forward anyway and works with you to resolve the situation. All obstacles melt away in the light of this team effort.

SIXTH LINE 9: Mistrust makes you lose your sense of reality and perspective. Friends appear to be enemies. Luckily before you act to defend yourself from these "enemies" you see your error. Problems dissipate and friendships endure. Good fortune.

The I Ching, the Book to turn to for Wisdom and Guidance

Joy (58) 066

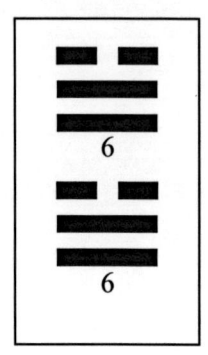

Upper and Lower trigram 6 Lake: joy, purity and truth.

Lake over Lake; things are remarkably in focus and clear for all to see. (Ideas come clearly to mind.)

An exchange of ideas brings progress.

Life is good and things are going well for you but you don't fully realize or appreciate what you have. It is fine to be happy and comfortable as you are but don't get be lulled into a false sense of security. This would leave you vulnerable to foolish whims and actions.

Rejoice and take pleasure in what you have and what you have already achieved. Joy brings encouragement and hope for a bright future. However you still need to keep working towards that future.

The superior man is very happy to encourage stimulating conversation among friends as this positive interaction can lead the way forward to a better life.

The Hexagrams

Joy (58) 066

FIRST LINE 9: With your contented attitude regarding your future there will be good fortune. There is no need to rely on external forces for all that you need to be happy comes from within you.

SECOND LINE 9: Stay true to your principles and you will not be tempted from your path by the distractions and temptations offered by the outside world. Your energies will not be wasted on regret or envy.

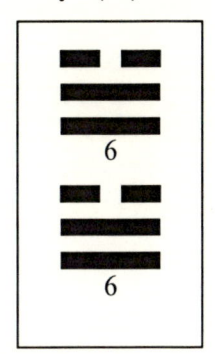

THIRD LINE 6: Misfortune comes when one shoves aside the real world in favour of dubious pleasures. These excesses can bring only empty, short term pleasure. A happy time hits a hiccup but the good news is that it is only temporary and joy will shine through in the end.

FOURTH LINE 9: You cannot decide which pleasure you want to enjoy. Take note of this and make an informed choice, looking at the pros and cons of all that is available. If the pleasure is positive and has some substance to it you will find happiness.

FIFTH LINE 9: Something you are thinking about getting involved with (a business proposal, a relationship, or religion) is not all that it appears to be. It may seem solid but is in fact crumbling away. Keep up your guard and be ready for a quick exit should the cracks start showing.

SIXTH LINE 6: You have cast aside your spiritual advancement and look to the material world and all its dubious pleasures to make you happy. You have forgotten that happiness should come from within. This leaves you vulnerable because your fate is reliant upon others. You may even be in danger of sharing their fate, good or bad.

The I Ching, the Book to turn to for Wisdom and Guidance

Treading Wisely   (10)   067

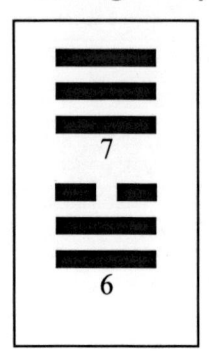

Upper trigram 7 Heaven: creative, active.

Lower trigram 6 Lake: joy, purity and truth.

Heaven over Lake; Symbolizes the love of a Father for his most favoured and beloved daughter.

Correct conduct is very important in this hexagram. Though you may tread upon the tail of the tiger you are not bitten by it. There will be good fortune.

The youngest daughter is wild and headstrong. Her Father firmly tries to exert his will. His love for her and her respect for him win the day and all is well between them once more.

This is a time of great difficulty and there are many obstacles in your path. Your wisdom and courage will get you through this if you play by the rules and keep your head down. Use your brain, think positively and don't be afraid to be creative when looking for solutions to the problems that lie ahead of you.

This is a time for deliberate action. There will be progress and success if one behaves nicely toward others.

The Hexagrams

Treading Wisely (10) 067

FIRST LINE 9: Now is the time for simplicity and truthfulness as you move toward your goal. Act with good conscience and all will be well.

SECOND LINE 9: This is a time for modesty, not pride or ambitious plans. Plod steadily along the path without making a fuss about it and there will be good fortune ahead of you.

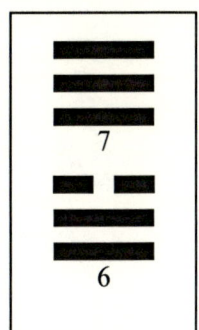

THIRD LINE 6: You have not been realistic about what you can achieve with your abilities. The project is too hard for you to achieve. Is it really worth throwing everything away just to impress someone else in a higher position than yours? This will fail and you will look stupid.

FOURTH LINE 9: You can tread on the tail of the tiger and not be bitten if you are very careful how you do it. You are able to proceed with a dangerous task because you know what you are doing. Proceed slowly and with caution. There will be good fortune in the end.

FIFTH LINE 9: The plan you are working on is dangerous. The fact that you know this gives you the strength and confidence to complete it successfully. If you are not comfortable with this plan, you must find another that is safer and feels right for you.

SIXTH LINE 9: Your venture nears its end and it is time to evaluate how you have done so far. In the course of doing this, you see whether you are on the right path. By looking at the good already achieved you will gain a snapshot of what the future holds and what to expect.

The I Ching, the Book to turn to for Wisdom and Guidance

Peace (11) 070

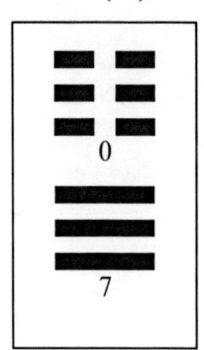

Upper trigram 0 Earth: fertility, passive.

Lower trigram 7 Heaven: creative, active.

Earth over Heaven: This hexagram is symbolic of good luck or good fortune.

This is a very lucky hexagram to have cast. This is especially true when it applies to questions of an earthly nature such as love, sex and marriage. Good fortune is achieved with virtually no effort.

Just as all things thrive and grow in the spring, the meeting of the male and female aspects of creativity lead to harmony, progress and good fortune. Bad things are going away and the good things are coming soon.

There is no restraint, all are free to mix and mingle at will. The superior man is in the middle of it all, his luck and fortune positively flourishing while those who are selfish, negative and unfriendly are losing their influence. Assistance is there for all who need it.

The Hexagrams

Peace (11) 070

FIRST LINE 9: Moves made for the benefit of others will meet with good fortune. Having a sound plan and like minded people working together successfully benefits all.

SECOND LINE 9: This is a prosperous time and not a time to be selfish. Think of others, helping them where possible. Tolerance and a vision for the future are helpful attributes to work towards right now. Be aware of the shortcomings of others and accept them for who they are, not what they may have to offer you.

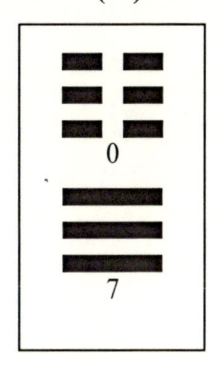

THIRD LINE 9: You must make the most of the present good times. Change is on its way bringing who knows what. Hold onto memories of happier times for these, your strength and determination will get you through whatever happens next, good or bad. Be aware of the danger remain positive as you face it head on.

FOURTH LINE 6: The end reward and wealth must not be your main focus any more. Now is the time to keep the lines of communication open with those around you whatever their station in life. The input of everyone is important now as all are working toward the same goal. Keep plodding steadily forward and you will get there.

FIFTH LINE 6: Others will give their support to your efforts because of your neutrality and sense of what is right in this situation. You will achieve your aim successfully by working with them.

SIXTH LINE 6: The expected change in fortunes has come to pass. There is nothing anyone can do to stop it, to even attempt to will result in humiliation. Now is the time to be like the wise fisherman who stays safely in port when there is a storm.

143

The I Ching, the Book to turn to for Wisdom and Guidance

The Restraining Force   (26)   071

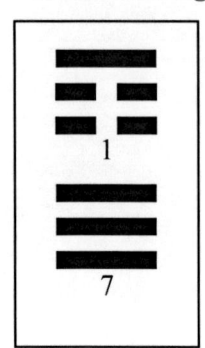

Upper trigram 1 Mountain: arresting, stillness.

Lower trigram 7 Heaven: creative, active.

Mountain over Heaven: power, wisdom and knowledge held back until the time is right to help mankind.

Perseverance is very important now. This is a good time to cross the great water or successfully complete a task. It is better not to sit at home brooding by yourself.

Be pro active and find a solution of your own. Be a participant in life, not a spectator! A positive state of mind and busy hands is the best way forward.

The superior man uses the lessons from the past to help him to deal with what is happening now. However, he must know how to apply it appropriately to help everyone including himself.

The Hexagrams

The Restraining Force (26) 071

FIRST LINE 9: This is not the time to move forward and surmount the obstacles that lie ahead. It is better to be patient and stay put in safety until the situation changes.

SECOND LINE 9: It is not a good time for advancement. The forces holding you back are beyond what you can handle right now. The best thing to be done is to pause and reflect on what is happening while building your resources back up to strength.

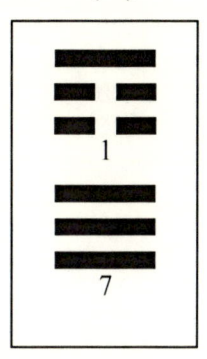

THIRD LINE 9: Be cautious as things begin to move again for you. Remain focused on your goals and think carefully before allowing others to join forces with you. Be prepared for the unexpected and all will be well.

FOURTH LINE 6: You are a stronger, better person because of the lessons learned from the adversity you have just survived. Your resources have not been squandered. They have become a strong and valuable reserve for the future. Meet your problems head on and all will be well. Good fortune.

FIFTH LINE 6: Weakening the enemy makes it easier to control. An indirect or devious approach to the problem is best in this situation. So don't waste valuable resources in tackling the problem or danger head on. Good fortune smiles upon you.

SIXTH LINE 9: There is great progress as all obstacles fall away from your path. Positive energy correctly used accomplishes great things. If you are respectful of tradition there will be nothing barring the way forward. All that you wish to achieve can be accomplished.

The I Ching, the Book to turn to for Wisdom and Guidance

Patient Anticipation   (5)   072

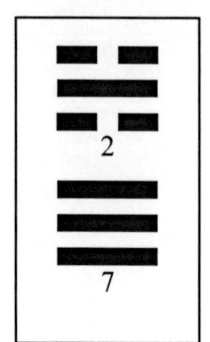

Upper trigram 2 Water: a pit, danger and chasm.

Lower trigram 7 Heaven: creative, active.

Water over Heaven; the farmer waits for the promised rain.

The air is ripe with the promise of rain but it has not yet started to fall. It is important to be patient and wait for the promise to be fulfilled, for the rain to fall, for the right time to move.

It is advantageous to cross the great water but one must plan ahead and get the timing right. When the time comes you must act swiftly and decisively. Then and only then will you successfully achieve your goal.

The superior man realizes that it would be a mistake to take on the imminent danger before the time is right to do so. Instead of acting now, he waits for that time and makes preparations for dealing with whatever lies ahead. He is rewarded with amazing success.

Seeing things as they really are is advantageous just now.

The Hexagrams

Patient Anticipation (5) 072

FIRST LINE 9: Although there is a problem, it lies in the future not the present. Now is the time to work on a solution. Fear of the coming problem must not be allowed to distract you from plans you are making for its resolution before it hits. An unplanned move now would leave you vulnerable to the problem before there is a solution in place.

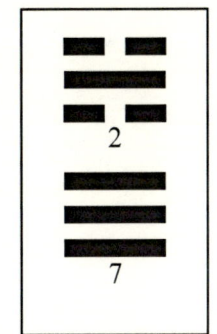

SECOND LINE 9: Your ideas will make life complicated for a while. You are likely to be the victim of scandalous gossip. Remember that if you do not comment on it, the gossip will have no foundation! Stay calm, keep quiet and your efforts will eventually have a successful outcome.

THIRD LINE 9: Don't waste your energies worrying about what is to come. Instead, make plans and find a solution to the problem. This way you will be able to cope with it from a position of strength when it happens.

FOURTH LINE 6: Stay calm, keep looking around and take a deep breath. Step back from the situation immediately while you still can! There is no way forward or back so it is better to get yourself out of harm's way.

FIFTH LINE 9: Take time to calm down and regain your strength for what lies ahead. The storm that is the situation rages all around you. All you can do for now is, wait until the time is right to make your planned move.

SIXTH LINE 6: The problem/situation you have been anxiously awaiting has arrived. Whatever form help takes, whoever holds it out to you, accept it graciously and all will be well. Now is not the time to be choosy about what is offered. You need all the help you can get at this point! The situation will turn for the better eventually.

The I Ching, the Book to turn to for Wisdom and Guidance

The Power of the Weak (9) 073

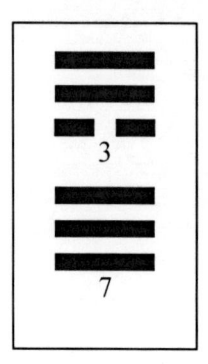

Upper trigram 3 Wind: wood, gentleness, penetration

Lower trigram 7 Heaven: creative, active.

Wind over Heaven evokes: a wise old cat that has learnt to stalk his prey slowly and quietly.

Clouds are seen in the sky but so far the rain has held off. The weak and small use what strength they have to restrain, slow down or impede a situation until the time is right to move once more.

Persuasion and diplomacy often succeed where brute strength would only make a situation worse.

At this time, it is better to think small when it comes to successes and goals. Don't try to take on more than you can comfortably manage in safely.

Gentleness and persuasion are the order of the day. Consider the needs of others and how best to help them. All this will lead to more success in the long term.

The Hexagrams

The Power of the Weak (9) 073

FIRST LINE 9: Don't use brute force to get past obstacles. Take a step back and look at what is causing the situation. What is its true nature? Think carefully before moving forward and there will be good fortune.

SECOND LINE 9: It is wise to retreat to safer ground while you take a fresh look at the situation. Seek guidance from examples of what others have done before when faced with a similar situation. Good fortune without endangering yourself or your principles.

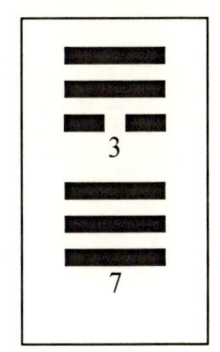

THIRD LINE 9: Although moving forward appears to be possible, all is not as it seems. If you blunder ahead with your plans, defeat and humiliation lie ahead for you. Ignoring the advice of the weak comes at a cost; you are humbled and proved to be wrong.

FOURTH LINE 6: If you are honest and frank with others about your own fear then catastrophe and danger can be averted. There can still be a successful outcome.

FIFTH LINE 9: Co-operation with another who is stronger helps you to accomplish your goal. The weak and the strong both have something positive to put in the joint pot and so further the cause.

SIXTH LINE 9: You have won the battle and now it is time be happy, rest and regroup. Sadly there is more to come. To continue forward now when your resources already depleted from battle would be a disastrous mistake that could only lead to misfortune.

The I Ching, the Book to turn to for Wisdom and Guidance

Strength of Greatness (34) 074

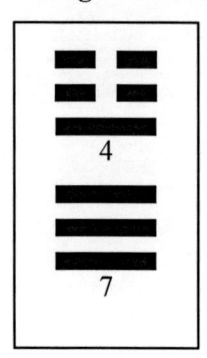

Upper trigram 4 Thunder: turbulence, awakening.

Lower trigram 7 Heaven: creative, active.

Thunder over Earth; the sound of the roaring dragon thunders through the sky, making the very air tremble.

This is a very powerful time like the spring when everything returns to life after the winter.

The situation you are asking about could be really good for you. Correct conduct is vitally important if you are to achieve the success you desire.

Although your needs are important to you, now is not the time to pursue them. It is important that needs of others should considered and factored into your current plans. Help them and they will help you.

Stay positive and confident about your goal and do not give in to negative or violent notions.

Strength of Greatness   (34)   074

FIRST LINE 9: Yes, you are strong but don't brag about it. The time is not yet right to make a move. You are not prepared for it or in a position to accomplish it. Trying to barge your way through on brute strength alone is a big mistake that would probably lead to disaster! Engage the brain before the brawn.

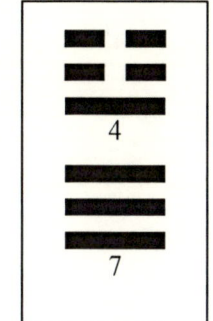

SECOND LINE 9: A slow, careful move forward as the way opens up is advised. This is not a good time to be arrogantly over confident. Make the most of your inner strength and avoid any sudden and impulsive moves forward.

THIRD LINE 9: It is better to be quietly confident and not flash what you have in the faces of others. Those who have not boast the loudest and fall hardest. Although you have power and strength, now is the time to rein it in and be aware of the dangers around you. A slow, cautious move ahead is better than not moving at all.

FOURTH LINE 9: There is no need for a great show of strength. Obstacles are more likely to resolve themselves when you use your inner strength and intellect on them instead of mindless brawn. If a ball of string is tangled it is better to gently ease out the tangles than to blindly keep pulling at them and make the situation worse. Work carefully towards your aim and there will be good fortune.

FIFTH LINE 6: A stubborn attitude is dragging you down. The situation is in hand and there is no need for an aggressive show of force. Smile, let it go and relax! Your work here is coming to an end.

SIXTH LINE 6: Progress has slowed down. Whatever you do has no impact on the situation. Acknowledging this will calm you enough to pause and reflect on the situation and the obstacles ahead. Eventually realisation will come that this can be resolved and a solution can be found. Progress can be made once more.

The I Ching, the Book to turn to for Wisdom and Guidance

Abundant Possessions (14) 075

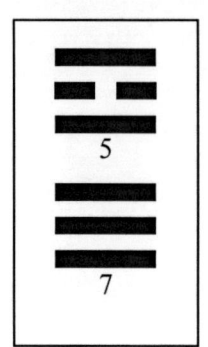

Upper trigram 5 Fire: brightness, beauty.

Lower trigram 7 Heaven: creative, active.

Fire over Heaven evokes; the sheer brilliance of the sun as it illuminates everything.

This hexagram is not only about physical possessions, but also about the wealth of the love and support that you have from those around you.

A wise person showcases what he knows is good and rejects all that is evil.

The bright, shining light lights up all that it falls upon. Although he is the ruler, he shows modesty and kindness towards all men. This is a very favourable hexagram and great wealth and progress are indicated.

It is reassuring to know that the situation will be sorted out. Help and good ideas come from powerful outside sources help to resolve the situation you are asking about. A mystery that has been puzzling people for a very long time will finally be solved.

Fire illuminates the abundance and prosperity that comes to those who remain humble.

Great inner strength and clarity give rise to a person whose authority stems from their great inner wealth. Material wealth and its trappings do not confer authority, they merely cloud the issue. Provided one shows kindness and unselfishness towards others, great danger may be avoided and great progress in the right direction can be made.

The Hexagrams

Abundant Possessions (14) 075

FIRST LINE 9: Your wealthy and powerful position has never been challenged or disputed so you have not the chance to make any mistakes. Remember that this is a new situation and there may be problems ahead. Remain true to your own principles. A wise man will not allow himself to be corrupted by his wealth and position.

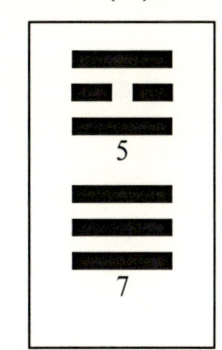

SECOND LINE 9: Your resources are plentiful and you are intelligent enough to organize them so that they work well for you. This makes it easier for you to take on bold projects with confidence.

THIRD LINE 9: Selfishly keeping it all for you will help no-one. It is far better to share your resources. Putting them in the hands of a leader or community who can make use of them to help the population at large! Most ordinary people are not able to do this but you can so make the most of it.

FOURTH LINE 9: Future mistakes can be avoided if pride and jealously do not force you to compete with those around you. Look only at what needs to be done now and ignore the rest for now.

FIFTH LINE 6: The people like and admire their leader. But he has to juggle with leadership and accessibility. The dilemma is that a leader needs to fair and kind to the people yet he still needs their respect and loyalty as he governs them with a firm hand.

SIXTH LINE 9: If the potential blessings and good fortune that are indicated here are to come to fruition there must be balance and harmony. Those who have wealth and power use it to help those around them. They in turn show their sincere gratitude for the loving help they receive in return. What goes around comes around.

The I Ching, the Book to turn to for Wisdom and Guidance

Resolution   (43)   076

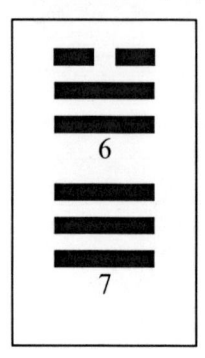

Upper trigram 6 Lake: joy, purity and truth.

Lower trigram 7 Heaven: creative, active.

Lake over heaven evokes; a farmer working hard to free the spring from the weeds that have been choking it.

Tension needs to be eased if there is to be resolution. There must be fair and honest judgement and resolution of an issue. Force is not necessary. It is advantageous to have a goal or destination in mind.

This is not a time for foolish or thoughtless behaviour. Actions should be carefully planned. Be kind and fair to those around you.

Determination should be peaceful, without malice to others; your intentions should be honourable at all times. Try to focus on deleting all the undesirable bits of your character.

Reform yourself but don't even try to change others. However, it would be helpful to be aware of what makes them tick.

The superior man gets busy giving of what he has to those who are in need. He is not thinking about his own virtues but of what he can do for others.

Resolution (43) 076

FIRST LINE 9: The most dangerous time of all is the beginning before everything is established. A mistake now could be a catastrophe. If you have doubts, now would be a good time to re-view and plan accordingly.

SECOND LINE 9: Cultivate your inner strength and maintain your caution. It is better to be constantly on vigilant with regards to danger than to be fearfully caught unawares when it arrives. Others, inspired by your strength and courage will willingly work with you to defeat the dangers.

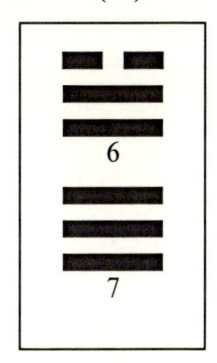

THIRD LINE 9: You must struggle alone if you are to win this one. To gain an insight into the problem, it is sometimes necessary to work with it rather than against it. Your actions will be misunderstood at first but people will eventually understand. You will not be blamed for taking the correct action.

FOURTH LINE 9: You meet with continuous obstacles but you will not give up. Although you have been advised to stop or step back and allow someone else help. You are too stubborn to heed the advice sadly; it is your stubbornness that is the enemy here, not the obstacles.

FIFTH LINE 9: It will take focus and determination to be rid of these powerful enemies. Like weeds in a garden there is a good chance that they will grow back. Every last root and off shoot must be rounded up and destroyed. However you cannot afford to spend all day weeding and forget about what you are actually trying to achieve on your true path.

SIXTH LINE 6: Although victory is in sight now is not the time to relax. Do not allow your guard or concentration to slip as you approach victory. One small slip up or distraction could snatch victory away from you. Disaster!

The I Ching, the Book to turn to for Wisdom and Guidance

Heaven the Creative   (1)   077

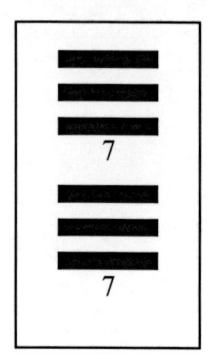

Upper and Lower trigram 7 Heaven: creative, active.

Heaven over Heaven; Friendly rivalry sparks off fire, joy and inspiration for all.

This hexagram represents the power of creativity.

A wise person adopts a balanced and well thought out approach towards attaining his goal.

If you go forward boldly the outcome will be a favourable one. This is the most masculine hexagram of all. Don't be surprised if power and aggression play big part in the solution of your problem or situation.

The superior man works long and hard to provide peace and security to all who need it.

Heaven the Creative (1)

FIRST LINE 9: You may have everything necessary to achieve your goal but the timing is not yet right to make the move. Be patient and wait for the right moment to arrive then pounce!

SECOND LINE 9: The time is right to begin your chosen journey. Seek help from one who is already established in your area of interest and work with that person. Your dedication and sense of purpose will soon propel you up through the ranks to a higher position in society. You will become a role model for others to follow.

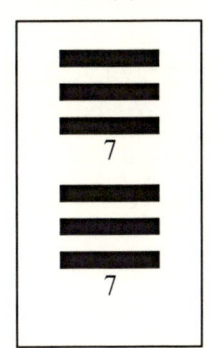

THIRD LINE 9: Stay true to what you believe in as you enter a new and creative phase of your life. Don't be distracted by the trappings of fame and success. Stay alert and be mindful of what lies ahead so that you can avoid future problems.

FOURTH LINE 9: you have some decisions to make. You have great creative energy and enthusiasm and must decide whether to serve humanity and be in the thick of things or to go into seclusion and work on improving your inner self. Your first instinct will be the correct one to take note of so go with that.

FIFTH LINE 9: You have very definite ideas and people around you are positively influenced by that. They will respect your judgement and look to you for help and guidance in their own lives.

SIXTH LINE 9: You have great ambitions but insufficient creative power to sustain them. If you continue in this vein, you will lose sight of reality. Eventually you will rue what you have started here. Take this as a warning not to arrogantly aim too high. It is time to be honest with yourself and know you are truly capable of.

Bibliography

An Edition of the I Ching printed in Chinese. This was a gift for our collection from a Chinese friend 1999. ISBN # 957 8909-80-2

Adcock Will. I Ching. A Practical Guide to Interpretation and Divination: Anness Publishing Limited 200, 2001. ISBN: 1-84215-227-0

Benson Robert G. The I Ching For a New Age. The Book of Answers for Changing Times: Square One Publishers, New York. 2002. ISBN: 0-7570-0019-3

Burr Rosemary. The Lovers I Ching. St Martins Press, New York. First Edition 1999. ISBN: 0-312-24082-1

Hook ffarington Diana. The I Ching and its Associations. Routledge and Kegan Paul Ltd. London, Boston and Henley. 1980. ISBN: 0-7100-0506-7 ISBN: 0-7100-0507-5 pbk

Huang Kerson and Rosemary. I Ching. A New Translation restores the spirit of the ancient Chinese text. Workman Publishing Company Inc. New York. 1987. ISBN: 0-89480-319-0

Johnstone Michael. The Ultimate Encyclopaedia of Fortune Telling. Published by Arcturus Pubishing Limited, London SE1 3HA. 2004. ISBN #1-84193-235-3

King Francis X. Encyclopaedia of Fortune Telling. The Hamlyn Publishing Group London SW3 6RB. Part of Reed International Books. 1988. ISBN# 0 600 557134 3

Legge James. Trans. I Ching Book of Changes. The Ancient Chinese Guide to Wisdom and Fortune Telling. Gramercy Books, A division of Random House Value Publishing Inc. New York. 1996. ISBN: 0-517-14990-7

Ming – Dao Deng. The Living I Ching. Using Chinese Wisdom to shape your life. Harper San Francisco. A Division of Harper Collins Publishers. First Edition 2006 ISBN: 13-978-0-06-085002-9

Moran Elizabeth and Master Joseph Yu. The Complete Idiots Guide To The I Ching. Alpha Books 201 West 103rd Street Indianapolis, IN 46290. 2002. ISBN: 0-02-863979-0.

Bibliography

Powell Neil. The Book Of Change. How to understand and use the I Ching. Orbis Publishing Limited, London. 1979. ISBN: 85613 063X.

Ritsema Rudolf and Karcher Stephen. Trans. I Ching The Classic Oracle of Change. The first complete Translation with concordance. Element Books Limited. Shaftsbury, Dorset, England. 1994. ISBN: 1-85230-669-6

Struthers Jane. The Fortune Telllers Bible. The Definitive Guide To the Arts of Divination. Sterling Publishing Co. Inc. New York. Copyright Octopus Publishing Group Ltd. 2007. ISBN: 10:4027-5225-3.

Wilheim Richard, trans. The I Ching or Book of Changes. Translated from German by Cary F. Baynes. 3rd ed. Bollingen Series 19. Princeton, NJ: Princeton University Press, 1967. ISBN: 13:978-0-06-085002-9 ISBN: 10-0-06-085002-7

Wing R.L. The Illustrated I Ching. The Aquarian Thorsons, An imprint of Harper Collins. 1987. ISBN: 085030 573 X

Woods Gary (photographs) A new interpretation by McCarver Dhiresha. The Photographic I Ching. Èlan Press, an imprint of General Publishing Co. Limited, Toronto, Canada. 1996. ISBN: 1-55144-119-5

I Ching Cards. Copyright 1971. I Ching Productions. Made in Switzerland by AGMULLER.

Gill Richard, I Ching The Little Book That Tells The Truth. The Aquarian Press An Imprint of Harper Collins 1993. ISBN 1-85538 029 3/7.

The I Ching, the Book to turn to for Wisdom and Guidance

King Wen - Hurn, Lookup Table

For those of you who have used the traditional versions of the I Ching. The following table; will let you look up Hurn (octal) hexagram numbers from the traditional numbers used in other books.

Wen	Hurn	Wen	Hurn	Wen	Hurn	Wen	Hurn
1	077	17	046	33	017	49	056
2	000	18	031	34	074	50	035
3	042	19	060	35	005	51	044
4	021	20	003	36	050	52	011
5	072	21	045	37	053	53	013
6	027	22	051	38	065	54	064
7	020	23	001	39	012	55	054
8	002	24	040	40	024	56	015
9	073	25	047	41	061	57	033
10	067	26	071	42	043	58	066
11	070	27	041	43	076	59	023
12	007	28	036	44	037	60	062
13	057	29	022	45	006	61	063
14	075	30	055	46	030	62	014
15	010	31	016	47	026	63	052
16	004	32	034	48	032	64	025

How to - Summary

1a: With coins take 3 'like' coins. Count 'heads' as 3 and 'tails' as 2.

1b: With dice chose 3. Count 'odd' numbers (1, 3 and 5) as 3 and 'even' numbers (2, 4 and 6) as 2. Tip: Do NOT count the 'dots'.

2: While thinking about your question, cup the coins/dice in your hands give them a good shake then toss them onto a table. Your total will come to 6, 7, 8 or 9. Repeat for each of the six lines. The first toss gives the bottom line and so on upward. Much like the floors in a building the lines of a hexagram are numbered from the bottom/ground up.

3: Traditionally; a '9' line is drawn as a solid line with an 'O' to act as a reminder that it changes to a broken line in the second hexagram. A '6' line is drawn as a broken line with an 'X'; to indicate that it becomes a solid line in the second hexagram. The table below shows how each line is considered in the first and second hexagram. As you look up the hexagram disregard the Xs & Os and just think of broken and solid lines.

Count	Line	First Hexagram	Second Hexagram
9	--O--	------	-- --
8	-- --	-- --	-- --
7	------	------	------
6	--X--	-- --	------

4. Flick the pages of the book to find your first hexagram; you will soon see that they follow a predictable pattern. You work up from the bottom line, looking to see if the line is broken or not; the broken lines come before the solid lines.

5. Read the main body text (on the left page) and only the text for your changing lines (the lines with a 6 or a 9). Note: If you do not have any changing lines; just read the main body text as your situation is for the moment stable.

6. Note the lines that change for the second hexagram. Flick the pages a second time but this time only read the main body text.

The I Ching, the Book to turn to for Wisdom and Guidance

Example I Ching question sheet.

Question _____

_____ Date _____

Background Info _____

_____

_____

Line reminder: 6 ——X——, 7 ————, 8 —— ——, 9 ——O——

Line	Count	First Hexagram	Second Hexagram
6	___	—— ——	—— ——
5	___	————	—— ——
4	___	—— ——	—— ——
3	___	————	—— ——
2	___	—— ——	—— ——
1	___	————	—— ——

Hexagram No: _____   _____

Interpretation of answer _____

_____

_____

_____

_____

_____

_____

_____